TOOTING IDYLL

VAL WARNER

TOOTING IDYLL

CARCANET

First published in 1998 by
Carcanet Press Limited
4th Floor, Conavon Court
12-16 Blackfriars Street
Manchester M3 5BQ

A CIP catalogue record for this book
is available from the British Library
ISBN 1 85754 333 5

The publisher acknowledges financial assistance
from the Arts Council of England

Funded by THE ARTS COUNCIL OF ENGLAND

Set in 10pt Palatino by Bryan Williamson, Frome
Printed and bound in England by SRP Ltd, Exeter

Acknowledgements

Acknowledgements and thanks are due to the editors of the following magazines and anthologies where some of these poems have previously appeared, occasionally with other titles and often in other versions:
Ambit, Blind Serpent, Cencrastus, Critical Quarterly, Encounter, Gairfish, The Honest Ulsterman, Lines Review, New Writing Scotland 6 (Association for Scottish Literary Studies, 1988), *Orbis, Other Poetry, Outposts, PN Review, PEN International, PEN New Poetry II* (Quartet, 1988), *Poetry Book Society Anthology 1987-8* (Hutchinson, 1987), *Poetry Durham, Poetry Nottingham, Poetry Wales, Rialto, Ripley Poetry Association Open Competition 1997: Anthology, Samizdat, The Scotsman, Sleeping with Monsters* (Polygon, 1990), *Southfields, The Spectator, Swansea Review, Tribune* and *Verse*.

Part III of 'Tooting Idyll' (under another title) was a runner-up in the First International *Stand* Poetry Competition, 1996.

'Rearing Its Ugly Head' won third prize in the Lincolnshire Literature Festival Poetry Competition, 1995.

'Sunbathers, Victoria 1974' was included in *Before Lunch* (Carcanet, 1986), as in 'In the 70s'.

for Francis King

Contents

TOOTING IDYLL

Mais soudain une rafale glacée venait rappeler décembre aux invités de cette étrange fête.

Le Grand Meaulnes, Alain-Fournier (1886-1914)

I

In the Garden

1. *In the Garden*

My inner eye truants from the living page,
via the elms, to soil, the source, the book
whose text we live: Galileo's 'grand book,
the universe', dimming any chained monk's
manuscript. Each leaf's metaphorical:
a hoarding . . . child's illumined cigarette
card from Wills. Light puts on flesh in white phlox,
Flanders poppies by royal blue flags, deep
throats at the red-brick wall . . . In Tooting Bec,
a shady bourgeois garden, reading on
in flaming June . . . dusk seems *de trop*. The next
tranche of translation for tomorrow's half

sketched, as *Germinal* grows under my hand.
I wait on your return from work, the light
rendered in our tongue. Swooning poppies cup
English peace . . . late tea in the garden, day
precarious as the hale ant under foot.

2. *Love's Old Sweet Song*

Merry, our friends ramble on bitter-sweet
about 'the inevitable decay of love',
inevitable as love's old sweet song –
some seasonal affair, a being burnt

like dead-heads at the garden end, year end:
one more . . . flower from life's clichéd bouquet.
I'd fly from them as from the Siamese twins
over the fence: a double bloom carbuncled
on one bent stem: one flesh, one life, two cries,
one beast with two backs rampant, raped and not

one thought between the two of them? Between
neighbours' *marriage à la mode* and friends,
wrily gathering rose-buds while they may,
we'll look to our trellis, whose rose half free
stands: rosy snow falls through this flaming June
day. Trust in our damned luck, despite the world . . .
Trust that our feeling . . . live another day?

3. *Over the Fence*

Long night, they do not see the sun go down

upon their cat-and-dog bickering (but
pets *don't*) . . . over the fence, through all the live-
long dusk. The tenor of our neighbours' life
dips flatter than a dead head: frumpy face
a petal, jackbooted under the man.

We always feel with the one who's playing mute . . .
yet, some pre-echo of her nagging, his

force . . . always hums when he's at work . . . Daytime,
she scurries through her chores in her yoked smock . . .
her floral overall. Long over . . . all

the orange blossom. Long . . . deep-yoked, white frock.
Shimmying leaves on our twin elms can't veil
their bloody war dance, blessed by Mother Church . . .
Are they . . . our dread . . . *memento mori*, toned
to keep us good? Until the frost,
you'll lift our window on the midnight clear?

4. *How Else?*

'Neither pursuer nor pursued', oh yes
that was ever my dream, so starry-eyed . . .
My airy arguments must have seemed so

windy to Rex in his Gethsemane:
'Who wants to pick each flower? Can't you be

less predatory? And less careless? And
surely, you want his happiness?' Alone,
big game hunter, he eyed me . . . not alone,
with fine faith. 'Rex!', later you were to sigh
'a butterfly flitting from bloom to bloom
and more! He said that all we need's a cat
sat on the mat, between our pet armchairs
– we're *staid*!' Beside the garden's open book

my desk outlines my life, grave, working . . . here
as in the old days. Yet, I'd never take
for granted your key in the lock, and breath
of Woodbine or frost in May. How else, love?

Dust

1.

Even the cabbage white's surrender flag
flapping across forget-me-nots, heart's-ease,
across the close June garden day . . . till all
the colours fade . . . reminds me: two years back,
sweeping the years' dust from your room, that first
time in this other life – pupating time –
I found it on the floorboards' black-stained fringe
around the foot-loose carpet. Flashier
than any brooch, filigreed red on black

– a little touch of hearth-light in the night?
Butterfly wing – Red Admiral? – its pair
pure dust. I left it on the window-sill:
the sun that lit its flittering, quick day
would quickly grind its pigments, too, to dust.
A sombre gesture, maybe . . . lighting our
luck beyond chance, till history end luck.
Or we fall through the garden's light-veiled ice.

2.

Together, we worshipped that butterfly
wing's filigree of *le rouge et le noir*.
'Darwin spoilt that, as token of our life
after life.' '*Would* you have believed, before . . . ?'
'*Would* you . . . believing Paley? Dear God –' 'Who

knows in another life, another time
and place . . . the old watchmaker's hand transpired?'
Reincarnation, resurrection, Jove
– we shuffled menus from shut restaurants.
'Even in death' – that flutter-by – 'it's fine,
unlike us.' Even then, vivacious mites
nibbled through '. . . what the eye can't see?' We stared
at that wing's Cyclops' eye, ground of dried blood.
Evolved through mud to grub, through dust to dust . . .
because you had responded, it became
more than a pretty thing I'd seen: our eyes
ricocheted off that wing's ripe edge, that tear.

The Caddy

The garden flowered on this grass path's stem
sets in the shade the hope I dared to frame
over my cups of char *du solitaire,*
gazing neurally subterranean
into the picture on the tin. That served
as caddy – pastel mock-lacquered on black.
It's on the kitchen sill, behind me now
as I lean on the house wall, red-brick warm,
waiting on your return from work. I con
Zola's double mined miners' words. That tin's
remnant of willow weeping in Cathay's
translated to our sun-dunked apple-tree,
in our corner of Eden. Whose rent's fees
for Englishing for such bourgeois as us,
as read . . . their underground lives, *Germinal.*
May the individual survive . . . the group?

Against the Wall

1. *Dead Wood*

June, rose Dorothy Perkins climbs to free
stand . . . living wood held up by all the nailed
dead, our trellis smothered by rosy snow.
Through tendrils' graffiti, I'd feared to be

cast . . . as the mistletoe on the tree, nerves trailed
over all. You took my free-floating fear,
fear of fear Bruce and Guy had so enhanced,
only confirming what I'd always known
tripping over my own liana nerves.
You took my hand and led me out; I feared
to be cast . . . as the ivy on the stone

wall (or it shores the wall against . . . itself?).
I feared to be . . . the shadow on the wall,
if not the bloody writing on the wall,
with nerves like creepers crawling over all.
You took my hand – as if that paralysed
princess behind the fake, the nailing briars . . .

2. *Against the Wall*

I lean against the house wall, red-brick warm
– loved like the electric fire's rose – through my shirt,
solid as snail-shell, brittle as white-washed
walls of Guernica.

This garden . . . we've lived here two vivid Mays:
the eternal return of the spring again
for us? I'd hovered on the threshold . . . dim,
a shadow chasing shades, till you affirmed
swallowing your quite biblical distaste
at sullying your mouth with God's damned word,
'Never fear, Tom, the stone which Bruce and co.
rejected is become the corner-stone.'
Your hand on that door bled from that red rose
we madly, sweetly dug in at the door,
a touch of Arcady in Tooting Bec.
Despite the world, we have been happy here.
We read the writing on the rose-nailed wall.

3. *Too Near the Bone*

A greener friend confided his day-dream:
pushing his love – young, 'well' and continent
– round in a wheelchair. He'd snatched him from death,
of course. I shivered then, under a cloud-
less sky (a peace-time summer day, that if

faithful die-hards, we'd have prayed last and last . . .)
The lamps'll go out . . . again. I'd vomit now
. . . starry-eyed, his sick dream was taking him
chocolates and flowers, the candles lit
before his shrine, his Lady of the Pain,
himself . . . paralysed by self-love. Too raw,
too unselfknowing to know that image blessed
his *laddie-ness*, less charming than naïve.
Too unselfknowing to know, even if
altruistic, even if you're in key
with the other's heart of hearts . . . what can you do
that isn't self-loving? But that is life.

4. *Convictions*

At least, we lived two years, two Aprils, two
springtimes, two lifetimes – one life. And who'd, still,
count time in quarter days with summer, still

. . . only four seasons off? Jack, Jack, you know
as near as dammit where you'll march away,
clear-eyed as I, seeing the road's dead end

in endless fertile fields of the war
after the war to end all war. 'I saw
a poppy flower through my skull – that split

against the shining marble-like white back

of the urinal. In that slow-fast split
second that's quicker than to tell' – third-hand,
Ray's brush with death again brought it home like
boyhood's shell of a man, armless, mindless,
who shocked me into pacificism . . . for life –
'I'd slipped on piss over the floor, was dazed
– he wasn't *tall* enough to be a cop . . .'

C.O.

Aged, he rears in his wheelchair, clobbers her
with arms beyond an able-bodied youth's.
But she's near-rubberized and nippy, knifes
– but his wheelchair's on caterpillar tracks:
Goliath mechanized versus the Girl
David, under a sable helmet. Flashed,
her blade's this sun-dial's hand; a hollyhock's
turned Wellsian . . . The nightmare woke me, else
dim dawn, although again we'd tired the moon
with talking, sent her down the sky. 'Next door
but two that German Jewish girl – things must
be bad for kids to be sent off abroad.'
'Refugees keep their health.' 'Their health
psychologically?' 'But Passchendaele . . .'

Pierced by white feathers not their bayonets,
I shall live loyal to his life, work on
the land . . . the land, yet where will be the point?

Drilling Seed

So in the end, you do break down and weep
. . . all of our fluids decomposing all

skeletal thinking, in the end . . . the soil.
The neural fire-screen meant only to guard
him from my fear for him blew in the wind
like some queen's hair embroidered on a green
arras, after the snows of yesteryear.
'I'd leave that corner. You'll not get much joy
from that shade.' Damned slip of the tongue? Not 'We'll . . .'?
I leaned, faint, on the hoe, he plopped puce beans
in rows, neat at the garden end, beyond

our little pocket handkerchief of green . . .
forget-me-nots to blue tomorrow and . . .
tomorrow and his life amid barbed wire . . .
trellised rose, red rose, wreathing us . . . last year.
His tears were watering the shadowed land.
I didn't touch his arm: the shrubs have eyes.

At the Dentist, April 1937

. . . As sharp as yesterday, run of the mill.
Gagged by the usual ironmongery,
stuffing my mouth. Half-choked, I understood . . .

the dentist's gentlest touch was an affront,
near rape. Boring my mind's bruised cells, his drill
rock-drilled a bleeding passage. And again,
all fingers and thumbs, he was bumbling round,
all his clichés on tap. Then that forked tongue
of lightning pain – the nerve jagged, my eyes welled
crocodile tears. Paralysed, my tongue wagged
narrating you the story of my life,
begged understanding. Craved mirage? Who wants
a doubtful gift of tongues, the forked . . . nude mind
fig-leafed by questionable ironies,
half-truths – *ah si j'étais un peu compris* –
doubtful asides, more doubtful images?
I understood. I craved your tongue's response.

Letters, June 1937

'I can't believe you'd not have written me.
After all, letters stray from time to time
. . . don't they? I don't trust my landlord; he sniffs
around the morning door-mat, like his bitch –
why bore you with this trivia, for all
it is *the ground of my being* . . . you know
you rarely leave my thoughts these days. The sun,
each dandelion dares me to live, each
passing . . . twilight, sepalled greenly against
the night, as people draw the blinds against
themselves. In that cliché of evening
light, poignant contradiction in terms, flared
among the clichés that are life I fear
. . . the bloody shadows lengthening each day.
It's not just politics, it's me . . .' 'I feel
the same . . . fearing tomorrow never comes

without that letter . . . oh I wrote, I wrote.'

Going Home, August 1937

1. *On the Char-à-banc*

Swaying through harvest-home corn-fields that bled
poppies, through dozy sheep, I leaned on you

in the empty seat. Long since, I had lost all
sense of direction . . . time would bring me to

you. Yet, in London I had mourned to see
buttercups replace the ethereal heads
of dandelions. All through farming Lincs.,
long wedding ribbons of white bindweed trailed
vows through the hedge. You'd kissed me: 'Visit Joan
as planned. The char-à-banc won't crash. We'll be

together soon. Your bloody pessimism!'
Happy . . . your letters my life, I would have
waited for ever and a day, yet feared

bright flowers changed from yellow into bright
yellow via gossamer: *les amours jaunes.*
Nothing ever stands still, except the old
fancy: change and decay in all around . . .

2. ***Going Home, August 1937***

With her ship's hawser slackened – long grey plait –
she sprawled schoolgirlesque on their cottage step,
old sandalled Fabian. The pair. I saw
their life, then mine – in Tooting Bec, alone . . .
the garden view: dandelions', buttercups'
recessional. Ken mourned his age, half-blind
. . . he'd found himself disenfranchised from Spain.
'You'd kill,' I'd said, 'the wrong people, the foot
soldiers, the people who only want to live

in peace.' 'They're my point,' bayoneting me
with his wall eye, through my Pisa-esque
slant to the distaff side. Under her breath,
'We're not even history's footnote' – Joan
smoothing her darned skirt over craggy knees,
'That's going home now.' Their shared life, my day
dream. But how to bear such hope in the light
of day? Fear . . . fear. Then, you met me half way.

Walking Wounded

Never again . . . walk to the garden end?
Our twin late springs, high summer, fall . . . to snow
drifts of tough bindweed that we couldn't bear

to kill, to save the weaker green things? Yet,
we took little for granted . . . yet, enough
to live here in peace, peace for our time. How
could we think that the world had let us be?
It never does. I lean on him to fight

the death blow of my fear for him, yet why
should he shoulder as well my bloody fear . . .

mourning himself? Yesterday, first light . . . Christ

. . . paralytic with fear, my spineless spine
their would-be sword between us. And he reads
my skin. We've lived . . . the dream. The nightmare spurts.
He'll march away, armed with my gift of fear,
his own: a doubtful consolation, love
to cry for, if they'd let you cry.

Into the World of Light

1. *Into the World of Light*

Saved by your casually concerned hand, this
weediest plant transplanted to the light
ventures a tremulous tendril to coil
round its stick, helically. Sceptical,
I wonder if it's worth so much of earth,
cosseting this anonymous thing, doubt-

less . . . less than flowering with *éclat*,
shamed by the hollyhocks' towers of red
and pink triangles, tapered heavenward.

March, I'd drifted out, 'I'm nothing without
the crutch of some text', some page in my hand:
I'd found you resurrecting that dim plant.
You smiled, 'Even translators have their day.'
The page in my cramped hand flittered to earth,
you picked it up . . . premature yellow leaf.
Sunlit, we went into the world of light,
into our bedroom, shadowy as trees.

2. *'The Enabling Dream'*

Was it your phrase or mine . . . 'the enabling dream'?
But don't our knitting thoughts often criss-cross
like creepers, writing on the white-washed wall?
Greenest of memories . . . flowers in this
green present, till politics take away
the grass under our naked feet. Twilight,
you'd draw close through your letters, through the ring
of lamp-light, fond visitant *entre chien*
et loup. We never asked the moon, we asked

all of a green while till the long night fall.
Even in absence, you would lift the day,
the everyday, tight-roped between *paroles*:
. . . so we translators may reflect light? So
the writer saying to her human muse,
his human muse: *Stay with me, could I face*
the light without my friend, close in the art?
How do you write the love scene without . . . love?

3. *White Nights*

Light like a cabbage white's surrender flag,
it was a long, light London night. Last week
after the heat of working days, and dazed,
we dilly-dallied in St James's Park.
Tram? You said 'We'll walk home' – ten miles? – shake off
the pollen of that royal park, through streets
of dust – no Queen Anne's lace nor loosened knots
of wedding ribbons of white bindweed strung
down country lanes, presaging peace, for all

. . . we barely needed translation to light,
given our Tooting Bec back garden's peace.
Our *nuits d'été*, searing frost . . . That day-
lit, foot-sore night we talked of Dante, Proust . . .
and like Francesca, talked no more. And soon

we'll talk no more, nor share . . . the light of day.
You'll march away to all eternity
– leave me . . . an eternity of *nuits blanches*.

Letters

Then, over white sheets, I would trail my life
through your fond phrases . . . mine. The pen would drip
all that unexpressed love, between the lines,
self-censored out of diffidence and love.
Now, in our garden where grand hollyhocks
totter, our early days haunt me . . . Past hope

flowered true as May, so . . . fears for you *this*
year, next year freeze . . . I flinch off the green

tide in our garden, stilled by that white pall:
the new ice age . . . Till then, your notes will be
censored by your hand, as if the officer's,
writing the things a man might write a man
friend – *of course*, so unlike a sweet wife's sweet
nothings . . . Where once we read, between the lines,
in lightness, shyness, understanding . . . love
– time frozen – only half dead, I shall read
in blankness, muteness, understanding . . . love.

And how long can they go on making love

a half life? *War . . . will camouflage our thread-*
bare costume parts of tenant and landlord.

That'd be my letter in a bottle lunged
towards a happier year . . . darker? The shark,
the submarine, lurks in the depths
of this green tide, garden gush where I wait
your safe return . . . This is the salty strap-

hanging hour . . . when old suicide still stalks
the garden – their leviathan's long shade:
their science, psychology, ethics, dear Christ!
Next door, their battle of the sexes kills
inquisitiveness. While a walk with Tess
down Drakefield Road casts her my *fiancée* . . .
A local idyll. We've each other, still

why act? *Why? Why?* – but that way madness lies.
We draw the curtains in two bedrooms – fuck.

Love

'Yet, love . . . killing the likes of you or me,
the common man?', cradling in my arms, still
my lover who will kill my brother . . . I

felt that you . . . understood I understood . . .
'We must fight Hitler or what's bloody left
for anyone? Anyway, soldiers go home

again', like Mark . . . shell-shocked beyond recall.
Mean time, I wait your safe return from work
– these small, sweet things – in our brimmed garden, brief
baroque of roses, foxgloves' steeple bells.
I'd love the man who'd ease your passing – Christ

. . . like Philip passing up his water-cup
as if . . . their war after their 'Great' War were
only another Zutphen, murdering

small scale . . . Small wonder my hand gets D.T.s
pouring the tea, as I recall old-school
Sidney like yesterday . . . your 'If I don't
come back, find somebody else.'

How Else?

1. *His Coat*

So now I've seen the future and it was
your old tweed coat hung lifeless on the peg,
another coat hung dapper on the peg.
So I'll throw out your shrouding coat, put on
the body of another man and feel

our universal pulse? Jack, Jack . . . *Oh Jack,*
that was another place, another time . . .
before the war. Again, we shall speak so?

I know so well that lived-in, threadbare coat,
that could be mine, slumping against the wall,
rinsed with our tears and semen, rain, sweet rain
– hung from the gallows, hooked on by my eyes.
My lily conscience nails you to the tree?
In Germany, I'd die more surely for
not fighting. You . . . Last time, some men came home
. . . not shell-shocked? You respect my ideal, dress
my fear . . . fear I just seek to save my skin?

2. ***How Else?***

In all the close . . . knit fabric of our life,
it could have been any day, and was

last . . . cruel April, condensation's cloud
over the pane. I sweated over clothes
squeezed through the mangle, through a Stone Age stench
of animal fur – wet. You'd hurried home,
your briefcase stuffed with clients' lives. The sty
on your left eye had flared a poppy, blown
by stubble. 'Conscription's coming closer now
– Churchill's "recruiting speech", *The Times* describes
his Mansion House speech yesterday.' No odds

. . . for you would volunteer, I knew. And I

– it isn't prison that I fear but that
. . . lily-white 'conscience'? Days were drawing in
in April, future . . . closer, and apart
. . . I went on mangling our familiar clothes,
turned one more ratchet on that damned machine.

3. *Never Again*

'I always see Mark in his wheelchair, moved
in and out of the sun, God help him. Jack,
looking back to their "Great War"'s blinding me?'
'Never again . . .' 'Not *that* way.' 'How else?' Through

the kitchen moist with steam, sweat and tears, death
stank through the air, as catholic as rain.
'For all they kill us . . . you still wonder if
one of our damned decisions counts at all?'
'Oh but you must believe . . .' I ached to kiss
away the unappeasable world. This spring

death was the voice's gentler, rougher edge
– the pea in our princess's mattress, your
bullet. You crossed the lino's scuffed chessboard
– our interlocking neural figure – trod
by spiders running our gauntlet . . . brief lives.
You walked upstairs, I mangled trousers, saved
one floppy leg caught up in that machine.

Feather Touch

Dear heart, your pale hand's feather touch will fire
. . . fatally into some loved body, there.
And was his father's death-bed in his bed?
And did he live a life, until the last,
or roam God knows beyond the pale like Mark
mewling in his wheelchair? What passing bells
in tinkling tea-cups? God's handmaids will nurse

crocodile bags, that two decades back clasped
sere telegrams, that cheek by jowl rub-rubbed
funereal confetti: in those jaws,
a white feather . . . a quiver. And again,

they will sip tea, knit for the war, the boys:
Roman matrons tickling fancies and threats
just as, 'out there', the purer man fell on

his gun, his trust. Is my misogyny
against my sisters since they do hit home
– white terror that a white dove's *billet doux*
highlights? Isn't grey doubt our saving grace?

His Shadow

1. *Towards the Garden End*

I know that I'll never again see them

daisies, not grave stones in that grassy sea.
Any one, his; and therefore all, his . . . all

of them, taken and cut out in little stars
to twinkle at us, who'd allowed them to go,
whose twinkle toes caress the good earth, their

common grave. But despite peace for our time,
how could you promise, given that your life
even in peace, may not outlive the day,
the bus? Or else your traitor heart may quite
outlive your love, dear heart? Darby and Joan
– that was ever the dream, more starry-eyed
than any star-crossed pair. Even a dumb-

struck youth cannot perjure the livelong day
by promising the life? Who wants to be
betrayed even by love's hand, keeping faith
with another *alter ego*: old self, slain?

2. *His Shadow*

Shading his shadow, burning in the grass,
where once I looked only for mine to merge
with his, against the backdrop of the green,
dyeing . . . fate's doubly crossed loving, I see
only a double stride-length into death.
The shadow is the Unknown Soldier's grave.
So what price now the war to end all war?
The League, the leafleted ideals? God

what 'greater good' than that each man should live
with his love? If the motherland permit . . .
Daisies that risked only your toes lie like
grave stones in an emerald isle. You'd not
damn even enough for a daisy chain,
which yet would solder too constant a link
for me, dying . . . before I'd hold you back
. . . a second, as your shadow chars the grass.

In the Rain, May 1937

First walk, Green Park, and hurrying through the light
rain, we were drawn under that chestnut. Bathed
in that fair-weather shower, we didn't fear
lightning. Your shabby Harris tweed coat kissed
my eternal alpaca, through the thread-
bare rain. I didn't fear being hurt, yet

inured to 'life' no longer looked to court
understanding. At your feet, I picked a leaf
glossed by the rain, blind fingers' vague star-fish
. . . veined life-line in Galileo's 'grand book,
the universe'. Recalling then, I'm still

rocked by the blessèd shock and May-fair rain,
bathing me in understanding like
on first reading . . . the page translated back
into the leaf light's *fraîcheur*. Yellow through
the dog days' weather-beaten and dun daze,
a leaf lit on your shoulder like a star.

The Sun-dial

1.

Here, at the still point of our greening world
amid the effervescence of the spring,
our eyes lit on the hand of man herein
. . . the face of this sun-dial, as lined as age:
hand of Victorian man in the face
of his fast, evolutionary past.

Still, we're pariah souls, amid pruned shrubs
and our pet plants, our little Eden here
in Huron Road, in Tooting Bec. With fine
disdain, your swallow-diving mind brought close
the empire builder of the house, who aped
the worker ant, tracking the Stonehenge sun:
'*Plus ça change, plus c'est la même chose*', left hand
near mine. 'Untouchable . . . benighted coves',
you shrugged, 'In their unsleeping eyes . . .', right hand
held out for any friend, whose shade you'd bring
– appeased? – into the circle of our fire.

2.

Bent to the sun-dial, as if kissing it,
you spun round, lectured sparrows in the dust,
their grubs: 'We missed our century – the fifth
B.C., Athens. What of Stone Age men's fires . . . ?
God knows' you smiled, with that grand carelessness,
embracing the anger that you dress with speech.
Here, in the garden, where you'll come home soon,
your hurt invective made pale roses pale:
'Run with the pack, while feeling with the prey,
standing apart while dog eats bitch, the best
of Christian gentlemen, so purely . . . a part

played to the baying circus mob. Pigs might
fly, oh men might . . . fly to the moon, before
they'd let us be.' How live, but drinking raw
clandestine eloquence, old as the sun
spearing your left side, that first day when you
bent to the sun-dial, as if kissing me?

3.

The wine-dark sunset shading into blood,
yesterday . . . merges into that first time
you came here, pored over the sun-dial's lead
face . . . under lead sky's fiery furnace. Then
the sunlight on the day, our daze . . . And then
again, next year, this year, the other side
of paradise – stormed by the looming dead,
you made it your bequest (solicitor
to the end . . .). 'If I do not come back, give Tess
the sun-dial' – how to move? – 'she covets it
so. Put something useful there – stone bird-bath,
say.' Then you laughed, I laughed, we left it so
. . . memorialized, dear God. Of course, I *would*.
Who wants a sun-dial drawing tides of blood

in melancholy, long, withdrawing ebb . . .
through shadow, dyeing . . . through my consciousness
since your hand trailed the sunlight on my face?

England, Our England

It hasn't happened yet, so maybe . . . Christ
half of me wants to live but for the day,
the live-long day. And mayfly-like to die

at the end of the blue-sky day . . . I've denied
– even after Czechoslovakia –
your last-stand vision, shivering at the mouth
of Hades 'where we shall go down. Or fight.'

If each worked in his garden, he'd not . . . be
back from war in a wheelchair, if he comes

back. Will the twilight dowse this garden . . . world,
the South Downs' speedwell, shrinking violets,
England, their England, where we walk with stealth.
Good enough to die for the land that locks
us up . . . for love. You'll join hands with the poor

'workers', lacking our education's luck,
locked out of the garden – no one's birthright –
joined with their 'betters' in spitting on us.

II

Over the Cups

1. *Bethan's Picture*

Dust to dust, a paper flaps from the tree trunk, going
home . . . to the soil we tore it from to read, to see

through forest clearings. Is it a notice
of some *nouvelle vague* or wind
of change or the name of the far away

house in the hollow trunk where bourgeois Owl lived
après Beatrix Potter or . . . ? Always a breath
of wind, leafing through the leaves. 'Stick it on
the old apple-tree,' Bethan begged. Through these hot days
of '84 blowing hot and cold, we've left it
there. Any kid's picture – an owl out on a limb,
a tree, a house, not unlike this Tooting Bec house
last in its terraced block of eight, the garden impression-
istic . . . version of pastoral, passing

good life. Is it a yellow ribbon tied round the tree,
pointing down the yellow brick road? In the window,
open, a story-book lies . . .

2. *Play Pretend*

Where do the pictures come from, pristine
as grass and the wild rose's curtain
of Janeite sprigged muslin, back-drop
for another *fantasia*, played out by the kids? On points
almost, Beth stretches to the grail

of the other's hand. They see. From the dust,
they open-cast mine the wild rose
petals – curling up and dying in hot little hands, faster

than fantasy can mutate. Wouldn't it be
nice to believe they're story-book children, without fear
or even *crises de nerfs*? Nice to believe this little
Eden here is all we know on earth, and all we need
to know, despite the dinosaur roar of crawling
cars. I turn to him, 'Nice to believe

we'll watch that fair head inch up the grizzled
Victorian wall, still standing up straight
even a decade from now.' We look

as if we read a future in the other's eyes.

3. *Over the Cups*

The sunlight dazzles me, like looking
through hair blown over the eyes, like Goldie-
locks: everything's fissured in the hair

fine cracks. An eagle, the moment hangs
'twixt cup and lip. I murmur into lemon – Russian – tea, not
seeing
the drowning . . . minute fly, 'If
every day were like this', like the day

light, the wild rose snowing . . . each calyx
firm, before lapsing. 'But it is

love.' And again, the cup runneth over. 'As for the weather,
this summer's near drought', yet who wants

a wind of change in London? He touches my hand, goes
to shepherd the kids to the train. Errands done,
he'll take them to St James's Park, to see
Jemima Puddle-duck at home on the royal lake,
the populace gathering where the wild things are,
faces merging in lapping water, whence we emerged.

4. *Look*

Against the banked pink-and-white roses, dog
rose, their fresh, unformed, pink-and-white faces smile
and fade. With luck, they'll grow up

with an 'English rose' look. 'Take Erica home,
afterward.' The kids' chat drowns me out, Fred's face
questions? *Take her home,* he intuits, lip-reading
my mind, nods. Conflated in the instant of a look, I

saw the child I couldn't know
. . . puzzled before the onslaught of the world

of the 'grown-up', the old man whom I could know
. . . puzzled before the onslaught of that world, him-
self. Or else laid out in sleep, after *la petite mort,*
stripped of the workaday self that is

the shadow of the death we hope to sleep out,
the shadow of the death we hope to elude, wrenched
by electrodes in a lost

. . . one's hand, putting the boot in on a flower.

At the Gate

1. *The Home Front, 'The Falklands' War*

Lobbing dead heads, madder, from behind
the rose, Erica bombards the others. I see her . . . two

years back, a-tiptoe on our threshold, apple cheeks
behind the Oddbins carrier-bag of Victoria plums
she offered up, sent by her mum 'to make
friends'. The apple of her eye, seeing

as she came to live here, virtually? The stones went
the rounds of the supper plates,
as the radio totted up the dead . . . *this year?*
Next year? Sometime . . . ? They still play
passé games. How can women

expect equality, while *England expects* . . . more men to die

replaying colonial wars? Unlike the armed men
sown by the dragon's teeth of Thatcherspeak's royal

we . . . the plum stones didn't spring up.
In their lengthening shade, we'd measure

our lives from the summer of '82,
a good year for Victorias.

2. ***At the Gate***
(for Sue Lowe)

The door clacks to behind them leaving
like a book closing: 'They are all gone into the world

of light . . .' baptizing me – with *The Castle* – in the garden
light. Behind me that long passage through the dark
house from light to light – the darkened hall,
unlike in Bede's bird flight. I lounge here . . . blessed

daze, un-English flaming June and quiet, apart
from the oceanic roar of traffic, that even
the adopted Londoner's ear cuts out. With windows
for eyes, the door's the mouth of the house
in the classic sketch of any kid, carried out

at the mother's gate, paternal threshold
. . . where the old-time bride was carried, waiting
at learning's lofty door before schooling
by life. And come the shadows

lengthening on the lawn, one need, one trust,
one secular prayer: may they return.

A Sister for Bethan?

1. *A Sister for Bethan?*

Even at two, the shadows creep up. In the end, they'll hang

from the Victorian wall. Mean time, they cradle
the pre-Clean Air Act bonfire patch at the bottom of the garden,
the fairies' old stamping-ground . . . with the teddy-bears
by the gooseberry bushes. The sun torches
a twig in the bird-bath, peeled by the kids and pale
as bone. We fall over ourselves trying not to

influence her . . . unduly. Jesuitical Freudians. Did the first
five years make Bethan? You dread brain-washing
. . . beginning with the amniotic fluid. For me,
it seems there was always Cass, looking after me, and then me

and Cass, looking after Clarrie: we were called 'the three sisters',
over our heads. Doesn't Bethan's placidity mean the new

child will fit in, will be another . . . sprig
of Virginia creeper turning on the grizzled Victorian

frame, mortared with sunlight, hopefully
not bringing down the whole edifice, with the wall
hanging from the wall, the shadow from the stone?

2. *A Hole in Your Pocket?*

She was burning money in the bird-bath
at the bottom of the garden. For my sins,
I could dine out on my last foster-child – whose
deprivation? So hot, we'd not kept the birds
watered. They took dust-baths. What mirage of crooning

or rap tapes – discos – T-shirts – cosmetics – flaming self
image that she didn't have . . . did she lust

after? What Day-glo advert nudged her . . . set the world
on fire? In the bird-bath that came with the place . . .
Two blue notes from my purse bought
her '50s classic *acte gratuit*, all her own

idea. 'Yet, why, Lise?' 'What's bloody ten quid?' 'Yet
we live almost frugally, not what we want

more' – our Tooting idyll – 'Fred's woodwork brings in
peanuts.' Some will-o'-the-wisp lit her tarn eyes,
I babbled on: 'And I don't earn so much,
teaching . . . not that money matters, Lise,' I bibled
for the pair of us. 'So, Kate? I burned your lolly.'

3. *Light My Fire*

Two white youths mooned round in the half-
light, one fag between them, ruddy pin-
prick. The weed was their life-line through the lilac
evening, masking carbon monoxide
and themselves. All cats are grey
in the dark. I felt their eyes rake me, going home
to Fred's arms. Then I saw her legs

light in the night, under the eternal
black skirt – my foster-daughter leaned on a wall
across the street, as a smaller schoolgirl would stop to caress
a pussy . . . In their circling arcana
they were cats, birds

in their display. 'You said you'd be at Tracey's . . .' playing
tapes, mooning over pin-ups, not out under the moon
hunting them up. Tail between legs, Lise slunk home
with me. Long-haired and slim in the half-light, we looked
like friends or sisters, as we are.

4. ***Memories of England***

What . . . will they remember? Never
never question, I ask myself in this rioting
Tooting Bec garden, with the dog
rose, my skin-pink, sister of the English official

rose, that colonized that world.
I'd shed light on the kids, contrasting them
and me – or then and me? Each citizen's 'past
is a foreign country.' The message of even London

pigeons peacably purring doesn't carry me home
to the five-tree woods of childhood's Metroland, re-
touched by Betjeman. While out in the country

each spire soared with the aspiration
of the homes it rose above. It wasn't the lying

finger of God in our image, crumbling dust
to dust with the emergent butterfly, free-
thinking teens. 'Great' War memorials rose to the noble
dead, not the murmuring, murdered multitude.

His Past, Our Past

1. ***The Jungle***

Through a tectonic crack in the crazy paving
I see a concrete yard I've never seen, yet

know like the back of my hand. It's warmed
by the *fiesta* sun, over our marauding
. . . green and riotously rosy garden. An ant climbs up the wall
of my arched foot. 'It's the little things finish

us,' Fred'd murmured. 'There was a backyard
at one of the places where I lived – subsisted – after Glenda's

death. A mini-concrete jungle' in his maxi-concrete
jungle of Poplar 'yet, through a crack
in the concrete, a kind of washed-out
bluebell, wan pink or lavender was labouring

up. I never knew its name. It was a flower.
And the next year . . . I felt I'd seen it through

and again the third . . . May. When the – *caprichio* – almighty

and small-minded landlord trashed it,
the dear green thing. It was my luck.'

2. *For the Unnameable*

'Things were against you from the first day, seeing
how moonlight-flitting and shady

previous occupiers had kept you under, treading
you into the ground. And "one does fear
they'd overrun the place . . ." *this year? Next year? Sometime . . . ?*
And then

again, you're Lilliputian, and positively swarming. And
I don't even know your name. Sure,
you've as good a right to chance

your arm, as the next person. I trust things
will go well with you in the great outdoors,
out in the night, out of my living space,
away from the carpet you cling to . . . at the hearth. Christ,
what if souls do transmigrate?' Glenda's dying,

Agnes' leaving him, the muddle of our old relationship, another

redundancy – everything floored Fred
in his windy bedsit, where I found him flirting
with ways of life, among the carpet beetles.

3. *First Walk, Last Walk?*

On such a day as this, who'd not look through shades,
darkly? Burning-lens afternoon blinding
the naked I, blanching memory like bones . . . We have

the interdependent life women friends dubbed
never-never or seen through

rose-tinted glasses. Through Everyperson's dark night,
I hugged a grass verge, James Grieve apple green,
Lincoln green, how England was . . . Those days

the grass sloughing off-white snow
was yearned after like *rosé* light . . . coming on the sky,
after the false dawn. My day-dream was walking with a Fred,
talking or no, across the common or garden
. . . municipal park, a few trees charcoaled

in . . . June. Always more straw than grass, muffling the
apocalyptic
hooves of *fiacres* . . . for the sick, down bourgeois streets

as merrily we roll along, twinklier-toed
than the haves at late Tudor frost fairs on the Thames, their cold
war.

4. *His Past, Our Past*

Through filmy eyes, I glimpse
the bedsits of his youth and fantasies,
everything centred on her . . . final nest:

one among identikit thousands, their
terraced house Fred loved, then hated so
. . . skirting the fatal spot, turn-coat
as the weather. And the first fruit:
the anxious waiting period, possession
clouded with contractual quibbles, a March
cuckoo, a commonwealth of plants
acquiring side-shoots and names, another kingdom
of the weeds. Cuba – they lived through
there . . . that was living, nail-biting
on their edge: *Give us this day* . . . security
. . . another week, year, all of our
chancy, unallotted lives. And still the orange
sunsets in the wine-dark sky.

The Afterglow

1. *La lune en bouteille*

A packet, slipping down the oceanic deliquescence . . .

Once in a blue moon, I'd broach that heavy-duty Manila
envelope,
plundering that kangaroo pouch of past, flipping

through papers – aged by old light beyond
our age – after some legal document, only meaning-

ful *in absentia*. God knows how it came
there, his Ernst postcard glowing blue

gentians and olives between gilded type-
script. A baby-face and drink-ruddy moon glares on
. . . a pre-Armstrong moonscape. In the golden moment

of this June garden, reincarnated as book-

mark, the postcard slips from Kafka's *Castle,*
from Gutenberg's world-rocking
medium . . . The message in the bottle on the moon

tide sings 'Why don't we meet sometime
if you like?', unsigned . . . but by his hand
on a Tate postcard, franked in Dover.

2. ***The Afterglow***

A daub of red and sea, a half-moon on

a thumb-nail sketch is a scorching stamp: medievally
illumined capital. The stamp's half-drowned
in franking ink, like Victorian historians'
'Dark Ages', stamped on Europe by 'barbarians''
soles. A tease for the Golden Hordes,
pre-punk tourists, the '75 Turner bicentenary
stamp on this old postcard bookmark (a lost friend
surfacing with that self's *timbre*) throws me

back on the Tate's light . . . aquatic galleries. In the end,
we'd withdraw from weedy Ophelia (drowning
in the willow-slanted brook,
in a conception more immaculate than any

Pre-Raphaelite nuptials) to drift back to Turner's
afterglow. With his light
of the world in our eyes, we'd wait on the lights
to cross Millbank to see the Thames flow past . . . to see.

Le spectre de la rose

1. *La vie en rose*

Unpruned, unkempt, the dog rose could soon take over
all. Heard in Huron Road, the traffic's some *passé* beast
bellowing from prehistory, or mazy

bee. I wait on heart-break Merle, while self-improvement waits
on me: *The Castle*'s unopened on my lap. And at my feet,
another kingdom of the weeds: Fred and I live

like two Canutes watching the greenery lap
our knees, *memento mori* sent to keep us whole
while fickle feeling serves our turn? Single

blush-rose petals float frail as a bride's,
not rotting on the stem like the incontinent
tea roses, only restrained by the dog

rose's saturation chicken-wire . . . How can you live
but day by day, making your way across

the ice? Even if Fred fell under a bus
this afternoon, under a dinosaur, however hell

opened, I should have lived.

2. *Le spectre de la rose*

'Why must you always want to pick the flower,
love?'

                In another world, she was hung up
on the tallest rose bush, trailing

. . . musk through the passionate short-term

that's childhood. 'Oh spare her one spray! After all,
there's so much . . .' wild rose, dog rose trailing clouds
of frailty. 'It won't last so long indoors,
Beth,' he counselled. 'But we shall see it more.' Beyond
the day? But from our bedroom's

raised sash, the ghostly roses

polka-dot a hedge

(of wire, with a silver sheen
les nuits d'été, in no man's
land)

of midnight Tooting Bec. While she sleeps,
hopefully with seven-year-old exhaustion and safe
dreams, we're entwined in a fairer
arrangement than Sleeping Beauty
. . . beyond the circlet of thorns.

3. *Ring-a-ring o' roses*

God, wouldn't it be nice to have believed in security
against even the Black Death? Often, we watch the kids, Salk sugar-
lumped against polio, processing . . . old magic in a ring. Limed

in it, childhood's the place you want to quit

to join the grown-ups, who are free. And then you want
to go back to understand your children, bone up on
who's kidding whom. But you've locked the door on your own

. . . child, throwing away the key. Beyond the magic circle,
beyond the wall, the morning glory, the grass,
Tooting Bec's street-wise, street-corner kids seek

to employ free time and fear . . . black
death, white death. *A-tishoo!*
A-tishoo! We all fall down. 'To offer a rose'
Fred said, 'that means to offer virginity . . .' '. . . going "naked
into the conference chamber."' We'd ringed the sites' eye-sore
at Upper Heyford and Greenham, embracing the

weeping sore, planting snow-drops.

Veil of Tears

1. *Veil of Tears*

In the June garden's green flare, a sparrow
fluffs out his unnumbered feathers in the dry bird-bath,
dust-bowl. Was Lisa's emptiness exhausted
after the soda-fountain of her tears, the day

she cried? She wouldn't tell me 'why':
some rebuff at school or romantically *en route*
home – the tropical storms of adolescence? What if

there's no end to *Sturm und Drang*, like sad friend Merle's?
Kafka's

Castle lies unopened in my lap, as if Merle were on time
for once this Mediterranean Tooting afternoon, out
of character . . . What fuzzy insights can I

rustle up? Not even dusty answers, to fire
with tears her evolutionary clay. She'll drag her life
here, smiling over her heart bleeding over her sleeve
over a CND badge. Bourgeois pain? – the miners out
three months. Tears only mask the sum
of negligence, 'bad luck', bad apples, nature, nurture?

2. *Bloody Tears*

Still down with flu, Lisa couldn't slop
at her school snail's pace through the zoo morning
of getting her scatter brains and the rest
of her together. She mislaid common sense:
to hold a fistful of tissues like a white cabbage rose
to her nose, with her head for once magisterially

laid back. Quick tears of blood inked her patchwork quilt
from the rose of the watering-can of her nose: an old hand's
labour – Victorian? – was wept over, in kind. Reds

bruised, white blushed
for bloody rubies through the broken glass
of tears. Twelve-year-old veteran of so many

foster homes. 'Nothing ever makes me cry
now' was an early remark volunteered us:
for that, she'd burn at the bloody stake, as I
for my belief half sickness is in the mind, knowing
in my bones blood's never thicker than water.

3. *Cotton-wool Legs*

With so little self-love, she seemed to like
her legs, if you could tell in the motley

of tights she'd somehow picked up: Lise lacey,
herring-boned, harlequin, 'tarty' black fish-netted, tartan
paraded under a strained black skirt
she'd not be divorced from . . . showing off old
young chorus-girl legs, till with flu the goddess stopped

pulling the strings that jerked her
on through the *trouvés* of her life's *déjà vu*. In my arms
she folded like a rag-doll who's seen better days, bound
for somebody's glory-hole, the rummage-sale, the dark.
Why was she so . . . long-term listless? Did she eat

her school lunches? Much mulled over. Much
fostered wraith, whom nobody ever stood up by the wall
. . . each year, marking her inching strides toward the grey

eminence of adulthood, our doubtful continuity
in a world of returning swifts and green seasons?

In the Cells

1. *The Prisoner*

Slumped on the garden step, talking closer
to the bone . . . Skull in hands, crouched to a crack

in the crazy paving, 'It's heresy
to say it', twisting a blade
of grass, someone, somewhere, would reach out

to eat before going . . . 'But loved,
even if it hadn't lasted long, you'd have lived
whatever face the world mooned at you, say as a prisoner

of conscience, out of the day.' Dead
wood the kids threw out for a boomerang
fossilizes. 'Not that you'd want anyone to wait out

the sentence . . . only hoping . . . if free,
he could salvage enough for another

love.' An ant on the step skirts
her foot. Does Merle see

it? Inside the cells, a harmless
insect's life to the prisoner, some-
thing outside the mind?

2. *In the Cells*

Slumped on the garden step, musing closer
to the bone . . . Skull in hands, crouched to a crack

in the crazy paving, Merle stares as if she sees
beyond the cracks lined by blasted weeds,
the slabs sluiced by sunlight, the usual
shadiness, somebody's dried

blood. Colour of plums. Last

summer, they came from the market. The kids planted
the stones, after the perennial *Tinker? Tailor?*
Soldier? . . . did the rounds of the supper plates. Merle

and Luke ate here one night-stocks-scented dusk . . . another
year and life. But for his porkies – 'but licensed for the field'
by his old divorce – she wouldn't droop in my garden,
    imprisoned
in the dream . . . *she might have lived?* Yet, we go on
. . . the progeny of old deceit and new
desire. Lying in in lying, how can humankind
hope, when in the cells we're so conceived?

Red Tape, White Ribbon

Tie-dyed rose, the bindweed unwinds
yet can't vie with the dog rose's
passé season. 'Why *did* you marry, Kate?' 'You can't
pass up your whole life, making stands. We wanted
to save any hassle with the kids', splicing white ribbon
to save any granny knots of red tape. 'Beth, I had

adopted, alone. But then we had that string of kids

here for fostering, and now I'm expecting

a six-year-old . . . sister for Bethan.' Each Christmas,
Beth cobwebs the place with streamers, tying us up
in knots. We meditate if she'll ever
cut the chains of superstition, seductive
as the sprouting maypole or bindweed streaking
ahead of us, before she breasts the tape:
the race is run through the Wars of the Roses
of red and white corpuscles, shades of the bridal sheet
as the cancer, genetically chained, finally flowers.

'Autumn Tints'

June rose, dog rose, wild rose's musky along the walk
as to The Paradise Garden . . . the Delius lovers'
end-of-the-world inn. 'Autumn's already

in your garden, Kate.' 'Autumn's always
the vivid season!' Smug. How long

has autumn been Merle's only season? In February, frowzy heads
yellowing on Brussel sprouts fulfilled
their natural end, wild strawberry leaves are fiery now
it's June, redcurrant, blackcurrant bushes orange
in high summer, with the flare of the dead

grizzling any season, against
an English green. Rusty like a broken ploughshare

all through the year, something or other's always going
west . . . And her eye lights on that, long before
the grand conflagration, the Red

Queen trailing a dun border, between
the red-hot poker plants. Sure . . . autumn tints
the prospect, after a broken troth.

Wallflowers

Wallflowers' hot scent is the old days'
breath. Anti-Armada crews knew the maroon

gilly-flowers, a tawny Tudor miracle,
a brindled blaze, spies' golden tongues among the brazen
court: fire-ships by land. Now, Merle on the garden step
bruises this clump's crushed velvet with her stone

eyes. Psychologically maimed by Luke, even while their one
in three shared weekends lived, she's lived on,
a teacher. And spectator – even the sunset sets the world
on fire. In her quiet way, a bourgeois
Merle would've lived an independent life even
a century back, governessing, *Little Arthur's History*
of England in hand? Now, she'd brake the necessary feminist
over-kill, innocent of liberation, like women who weren't

wallflowers . . . sitting out the dance, at every dance,
breathing attar of roses and ashes of violet, hot
on the scent of what they didn't know.

Butterfly Ball

Any chit-chat with the clinically sad's
breaking a butterfly on a wheel. Yet, the purple
passages of silence delude . . . I see Lise at thirteen, trailing
a shocking pink jersey like a cliché broken wing

and mute beside the purple-tongued butterfly bush,
flattering our senses. Till flowering with light
that night, as if God lit one of His candles
on next door's chestnut tree. Or blowing
in the wind, a freak Chinese lantern
set the world on fire . . .

The burning bush
caroled with every golden tongue. Fire flew
where even early '80s butterflies had fluttered by
– even a Painted Lady, if not our local *émigré*, Camberwell's own
Beauty? The little common weal between stinging
nettles for pupation and buddleia nectar was scorched
earth. So much . . . we'd not cleared with our arsonist. *Purely*
as a light show, didn't the bombs over Coventry hit home?

Burning Bush

'Lisa's handiwork faded.' The greenery papered over that gap

where the buddleia burned, through to the wood
green heart. Had Merle read my mind, out of her depths . . . ?
My stare abrades the spot, rubbing

. . . rubbing. Wild-firing over
all . . . merciful chickweed covered up scorched earth.
Come April, the wild rose weighed in,
rampant. Spurting into the bird bath. Then pink snow
exhaled musk. 'Fred had stopped her pestering his friend, chain-
smoking . . . for a light. At twelve. After dark,
we saw the garden flower with light. She burned

the butterfly bush.' As if quoting the *démodé* Good Book, I recap
to fill the gap: 'The blessèd social worker said, "How can you
give

house-room to an arsonist?" I said, "We've survived
so far." She said, "Quite",' at petal fall. '"A tricksy
age . . ."' What isn't . . . ? What could you say, even a Day-
glo afternoon in fire-eating June, to paper over that gap?

Bear Hug

1. *Bear Hug*

. . . *Next year? Sometime . . . ?* If we survive? I see Merle
at summer's end, on the threshold, looking out
over the rust-grizzled garden bleeding hips
and haws, harvest and death, where 'everything has burned,
and not quite through.' Poppy-bosomed June embraced
by smouldering autumn. Waning, the year'll burn
out, before the hoarding and hibernating. Out in the country

they'll be firing the fields, stubble and small wild
life, prised from low nests and running

scared before the wind of fire. '. . . Better
the most *louche* and predatory wolf

whistle. At least the heart's in the right place
– after the honey-pot! – unlike with a giant koala
like Luke with his promiscuously indiscriminate and fond
bear hugs, smothering your very soul.' What hell could
burn vivacious as uncertainty's pricking
flushes, fuelling the fire she can't know

if he doesn't mean?

2. *Dancing Bear*

With bells on her toes . . . a little gilt chain
on her sandal, she shifts her stance, one foot
out on the garden step and an ant goes

west. Human, the goddess shuffles again, rattling
the ball and chain of old heart-break. Anything
binds you, like cobweb threads

bejewelled by dew in my kids' sharp eyes
or old tears. Who knows how short

a chain a dancing and paralysed bear is on? *You have*
nothing to lose but your chains but
the self is genetically chained. We come
on stage kitted out with balls

and chains. Merle rattles on: 'People like Luke have had it
all – kids, the lot. He can keep on, bear

hugging humanity at large, but some of us, older, have not

started yet.' Who has the heart to murmur
'nor will', even in the sanctuary of her own heart?

3. *Tea in the Garden*

So English, 'Have a cup of tea' I say, force-
feeding her lack of love. 'It's all but

three. – Or a drink?' '"And is there honey still
for tea"!', her grave glance snuffs the chink of cups,
glasses, as if only a sip could transubstantiate
a past, better . . . not resurrected

à la petite madeleine? Or else she sees not spindrift rose beyond
the inner harbour's herbs, but Luke and light . . .

herself here with him. Like Channel firing (Marianne, pink
lion and Russian bear . . .), I hear the prehistoric
roar of traffic from Balham High Road, Sellers'
'Gateway' to the mythic south. In the no-man's-land

between her lack and my return of love –

Fred home soon – I duck her ravished face, eye-ball the dog
rose. If we're our sisters' and our brothers' keepers,
how can we keep the no-hopers keeping on, short of mounting

a round-the-clock watch . . . ignoring the hand's tic?

Autumn Pets

Gently, gently, with the flat of her hand,
Merle's seeing off a money spider abseiling
down from the lintel, framing her against my summer

garden threshold: 'Spiders are pets, practically
twining around the heart-strings, through the year's

twilight. They live with me a while and then
they go. I dread to think just where they go,
sprung from a mouse's black hole or whitewashed sky

to a Giant's Causeway of crumbs or worse
along the wainscot, or the unspeakably sheer face
of a *Guardian* in a tent on the floor. Mean time, they know
their place and stay there, moving a foot

a day, before they disappear
as if disappeared . . .' Alone, she's a prisoner in the cells,
hormonally. Yet, her pores suck this gilding sun. In all

conscience, what of the prisoner in the cells,
whose world's . . . the motion of a flea?

Beyond the Fence

Roaming through rain and light, the dog rose pours
pollen, petals, heaven . . . scent over our neighbours'
derelict fence. Is there ever an innocent

lattice, whose bars do not dissect
the eye, exiling the vision
of the day . . . ? Was it my dream or his? It became both

through history and affinity. One
or other shady subconscious threw up
an image of our fears. Redeemed by chance,
we ghost for the ghosts of lives that might
have been . . . plagued by phantom limbs, not cut
from me – escapee from suffering, except for all
the small crises to which humankind's heir. Quick

years together, we've lived the day-long year-
long hope, precariously, 'everyone's wildrose?',
beyond fair shares, beyond natural justice,
beyond the spoil of the law of our jungle?

III

'My wall, my washing-line'

England is falling over that wall, pink
like blood and pus mixed . . . with toil, tears and sweat:
dog rose, June rose, an unofficial link
. . . musk-roses, or from eglantine, well-met
with some old hedgerow cross. She ghosts my eyes
beyond the pane, pleading . . . 'We didn't see
her pinning petticoats and knickers high
up on the thorns – a crowning pair was tree'd –
night of the V.E. anniversary.
Tess, sweet old soul next door, not touched . . . *to see,*
screeching "My wall, my washing-line"!' 'Not pissed?'
'Her . . .' 'Hell to have the past thrown up now.' Blessed
heirs to their journey's end . . . their light, and missed . . .
Like broken glass a-top a wall – *a prang!* –
there's dew on the dog rose, rain or shine,
as they go shuffling, singing that they'll hang

. . . hang out the washing on the Siegfried Line.

To Pass in the Street

'My grand-dad fought in World War II.' The rose,
camouflaging their broken-backed wall, slides
in pink buds round our tea-cups . . . and the hose
of Tudor Hilliard's sad youth . . . 'He died.'

A spurting sucker trails into trip-wire
. . . peaty eyes soulful under black grass hair,
'before my time': sympathy not required.
'I would have been a C.O.' In the air . . .
her modish empathy turned on to bless.
Don't fence me in. Because she thinks *I am*
(my girlish lisp, my limpish wrist, born ham!)
she doesn't see desire under my dress –
oh fuck, play up! play up! and play the man!
And quip 'Still sleeping with the enemy?'
'Ken's of another kidney' – toe to crown:
'the die-hard's whoever doesn't see *me,*
Lara, when I pass in the street – but *brown.*'

Tess in the Evening

Out in the Russian-tea late evening light,
last sun on mauve Victorian villa bricks,
homes for those rising bourgeois still not quite
there, fronting the common . . . Doesn't it click

– a camera shutter, old Brownie box –
the figure reading upstairs next door framed
by this dying midsummer light that maims . . .
she is the neighbour Lara dubbed 'old crock'
(the other side of . . . four hours' tea, chat, wine)
tip-pling over the edge on V.E. night

May '95. '. . . loner, worked near the Rhine,
post-war. Tess roamed . . .' Her black-out of near night's
raised on the coupled world . . . With cup – slow mode,
I feel her lick . . . A dumpy, Vick-y mate.
Everyone needs to get pissed at some date –
walking on up foreshortened Ryde Vale Road,
toward the one-time new eighties' estate.

At the End of the Road

Look down old Huron Road, straight as a die,
toward a Tooting ultimate green peace,
pocket hanky of common . . . summer's lease.
Rose bricks patchworked in paving slabs have dyed
dusk, deeper *rosé*-rinsed by madder walls.
Against their one-time home, Kate's birdbath's hauled
– dumb womb. Things fall apart . . . the frosty years.
Visiting Lara – new friend – brings me here.

I saw the Startrite ad set in this street
– two fifties' kids putting their best shod feet
forward along *Life's Road* . . . Grown Fred and Kate,
through woods that could converge, too dark, too late –
Freudian more than Dantesque, old cold war?
A Heaver board points heavenward, next door
For Sale. The Heaver who built on Elms Farm
– here – was shot down . . . Dorking, by bro-in-law.
So Kate: 'We're not Victorians, bearing arms . . .'

Message in a Bottle

Through reverie's traffic, years' buzz beyond
. . . a neighbour's rocking tranny. I homed on
an empty laid in clover and fern fronds

to liberate the immured fly, that shone
. . . a top, winged out of faerydom. No bets
he was intact, would live a mayfly day,
if not a ladybird's? – the Virgin's pet
permitted in folklore to fly away
to save her children from our God's wild fire.

Common or garden, that fly was burnt, shocked
after a pick-me-up of flat fizz? Dire,
as ruddy Dandelion & Burdock socked
him sucrose of *le vin du solitaire* . . .

No Molotov cocktail, under the rose.

Pop! Hit . . . exploding Arcady's lost air

or Eden's sizzling snake . . . Under Kate's nose,
I tipped the bottle on their bed's Peace rose.

Balham Underground

A star, a coin, a bite winks at my feet
the false night . . . platform of the underground.
I bend to see what my slopped sole has found:
tan . . . apricot picked up in Hildreth Street
market. A black girl near tracks down my stare.
Her voice – not hers, the air's – deafens my lugs:
You crush what for us wasn't even rare
the war-time years, for all we dug. And dug
to dodge defeat. And death . . . Death's never fair.
Foxes have holes and those birds of the air . . .
What 'human rights' for those who died worms, mad?
Only the monstrous writing off . . . *Bagdad*
'shelter' and . . . Balham tube, a little Somme,
shitty landslide of autumn '40's bomb.

The train will come and save me from the dead
who held the line for three months, in stone beds.
Save me from all that . . . baby-boomers dread.

The Lost Decade

'God, anybody can lose a decade'
I'd breezed in which drab transport café, drab

bar? 'God, after all, Mrs T. did.' Afraid

of late eighties' tomorrow, Lara'd nab
fag-ends of crisps that somebody had left
– each time I met her, she was more bereft
until her new man magicked her . . . down south.

We'd met in pubs, venues for gabby mouth
or lonely mouth to have its bloody say,
price of a pint or Battle of the Somme?

Remembered now as this train bores away
northward from Balham, like Moorgate stamped on

some hearts. Some bomb, some crash took their next last

next breath – you know – dear – second – no – no – love.

(The lost domain,
all our Yvonnes outcast
beyond the greying pale . . .) Push come to shove,
what blondie did 'we' vote in peace . . . to blast?

The Cardinal

My local . . . dusk, The Cardinal, a stone's
throw from that mock Byzantine Brit-pink brick
road up to heaven's jaundiced flesh – and bone
of one-time *à la mode* cathedral. Quick

off from our (*good friends*) gossip's starting-blocks,
he'd asked about my long-lost Barry M

A thesis? (First – top – Army female doc.)
His jacket shrugged – I could've touched the hem,
trailing the vacuum of Westminster's bawl.
He said 'Who'd live like that today?' Enthralled?

'. . . Oh no? You could . . .' It had a dying fall . . .
Fred was already tilting up his half,
that said it all . . . home to his other half.

(James Barry found female was her death's sting.)

Drink on the record? Say, bound to keep . . . mum?
The couples never grovel for the crumbs
lonelies live by, stooping to kiss their rings.

Spin

Twirling the tankard on the table . . . see
its glass rectangles like a galleon's sail

– or else a coaster on that glassy sea,
a decade back, this pub with Fred. And flailed
as he walked out into our schizoid Lon-
don. Done. 'Who'd live like that today?' Appalled . . .
I was so strained by Fred and all his come-

on. Loyalty to Kate held us, enthralled?

Everything spun, the bar and I – not I.
The cardinal flap-flapped . . . a puce fuchsia
hunching to heaven, up on his sign, high

à la Arist. Bruant at Eldora-
do, on Lautrec's poster. Fred tossed a hand-
ful's wanna-be-Judas silver change down
– will o' the wisp on the bay table land –
'Have one on me!' He didn't understand.
One silver queen spun on, and I'd skip town.

Swanning

The darling silver heads and tails swam, spun
beside the brown- and blue- and green-backs stacked

up in the till. So I'd made it? In sum

a mattress, old York hippy's mat floor – shacked
up down the Shambles with some friend of Kate,
who'd scrawled a number years ago and said . . .
I called and said 'I'm Mark, we had a mate
way back . . .' *Mark*'s two a penny. Bread for bread
from part-time working in The Dirty Duck
or some such twatty, twitchy, birdie name
– I felt I wore a see-through frock . . . With luck . . .
(the Minster singed when Bishop Jenkins came . . .)

Until I heard the glasses go like crocks
and saw the man . . . new Goya's *Third of May*,
white T-shirt crucifix. And ran away

– if I'd charged in their fight, clothes could come loose
– they could've seen the mock cod-piece of sock.
Out of her tiny mind, the fucking goose.

Dogged

No ducks in those farm-yards – but the odd goose . . .

from whom I flattened myself on the air,
flatter than that will o' the wisp through spruce
that any pub . . . beside a churchyard flares,
fatter than that Hiroshima burnt wretch

etched on a wall, breathing down all our necks.

. . . My goofy transformation, door to door
selling tat oven-mittens round Yorkshire farms:
flinching at facing down each doggy roar
though unlike Master's, eyes were often tarns.
– *A job for a grown man?* Mr's or Mrs' scorn
as if the man had fallen out the moon
('This man, with lanthorn, dog, and bush of thorn . . .')
One dog sniffed up my bush, panting to spoon
– no speciesist, fast on the scent, but missed
slumped on my peddler's pack, *the black dog*'s list.
And playing my male half, my flapping fist?

Home Movies

Way back, tears rinsed the technicolour June
garden, with hay heat haze of Monet's foam

of poppies' blood . . . A man and child would soon

walk down that grass path . . . Fred and Bethan home.
Kate blessed not leaning on day . . . dream, that lit
up 'lost domain'. Up against that brick wall,
my skull, 'Luke can live in the past, *play it*

again. Home movies, mind' – as if I'd bawled,
Kate stared – 'he's only got to plug himself

in memory . . . only connect.' 'Maybe
painful?' 'He wasn't born yesterday, elf-
in never-never . . .' 'Memory might be

a strip cartoon – *Mad Magazine*' – cunt, stuff
yourself – 'at best, old thoughts in monochrome

ballooning in fleecy clouds, over fluffed
moments . . .' 'Kate, some of us've had enough blown
precious moments . . .' To star death's harvest home?

Oberon

'*Beloved Enemy* – won't They put on
that Troubles film? That Northern Ireland cease-

fire . . .' 'Thirties' Hollywood! Merle Oberon
starring.' I jerk off past . . . my name released
on someone's tongue here in The Cardinal
with Mirrie, Kate, Fred, Luke . . . recessional.
Why 'Merle', Dad? Now a pint-sized me plays Bo!
I saw The Scarlet Pimpernel *in – oh*
before the war, Wuth'ring Heights . . . *'39?*
Merle kind of stayed with me all through the war.
Live shots . . . Her fucked and fucked. (Lone or paid for?)
Tobruk and back to Bow's peace-time front-line:
hospital porter, humping to and fro
the semi-comatose. Plus wife – mum – woe.

. . . In school, asked of what's Oberon primo?
'Of never-never . . . ?' 'Fairies!' teacher'd screamed,
'Merle, learn by heart from *Midsummer Night's Dream* . . .'

Miranda

'This is the heart of England' Mirrie used
to tell her roses and her servant, yours

truly, in Warwickshire: 'Arden near fused
with Eden.' That such types are . . . ever more?

Thanks for that job through York Jude's old mate, Hugh!
His richly widowed aunt. I'd claimed to be
'an English teacher made redundant.' True.
Muscled in on her garden . . . husbandry
– eight years, *driving Ms Mirrie* . . . odd jobman
until she upped her sticks, tipped me two grand,
flit to her Jo'burg son via Milan.
Her rands across the sea . . . Never a hand
to blur the mirror of my bay. So cold

quizzing the glass – a lost decade? So sold
on her . . . snow hair, le Grand Meaulnes' girl, blonde *fest.*
I never told my love, Miranda, old
Land Girl, land girl, on that path going west.

Nick

Under the spreading chestnut trees and elms,
the path went on for ever and a day
. . . on, on, over the hills and far away:
a ruddy russet, maroon-toning realm,
the idyll that is . . . always round the bend
where they are singing still . . . world without end.

St Nicholas's church is blurred, though plum
on *Church Lane, Tooting 1841,*
a sepia wash drawing by E. Bell. Fed
by luck, like us . . .

That ruddy card has bled
out of my slim-line wallet, years . . . *love, Fred*

and Kate. Re-forwarded to Mirrie's. Fey?
Sold by 'the brighter borough', Wandsworth! May

. . . June once, with Luke, down Church Lane, hand in hand:
'A Saxon church sired this Victorian pile.'
'Hell, love, old Nick has always ranged the land,
car-exhaust dragon breath slaying the miles.'

The Sound of One Voice Harping on

Here in this corner of back-water West-

minster, two puce frocked cardinals hang back

to back . . . The two-faced inn sign outside clacks . . .
my Thumper heart, where Kate's Tooting card nests
love, Fred and Kate . . . love Fred . . . Does he still haunt

this pub from good-cause Commons lobbying?
Up from Kent now, and Kate? Move on. Can't . . . flaunt
a half a pint all mourning . . . evening.

The story structure's binary. Alone,
whatever sex, you're dim, dull, dumped on, dead.

'The figure on your N.I. card.' Dear Fred
on 'self'! If Mirrie'd noticed me . . . Moan, moan.

'If I'd noticed that socking bloody stone,
digging our bean row . . . My foot! – damned fork skewed.'
Bloke met with Luke, once . . . Tooting's Mitre – stewed.
In Attlee's '45, fifty. *'That clown!*
. . . I laid tramways all round . . . down Totterdown . . .'
until the lines meet in blue-sky fair-do's . . .

Figures

Still, in the pub the people come and go
talking of Michael Heseltine, *the man*
– '*après* damned Thatcher' 'Major limbo' 'So!' –
born to be top dog. Bow-*wow*! Or they plan
lottery life-styles, given all to spend . . .
where blow it or be blown but not be blown

away – *schtum*, round the Westminster S-bend
begging? While they commiserate, high-flown,
re. eye-sores . . . 'How about a mass of white

phlox in that corner where they say twin elms
stood till Dutch Elm Disease killed *ours*.' '*Quelle* blight!'
Two doves sip *Radio Times*'s garden realm
– ads . . . dream the good green bourgeois' nine bean rows.
One's visibly pregnant, standing to go
– no tacky Malthus sums in their green world –
that magazine in that belly bowl's furled:
'V.E.' commem. issue, weeks . . . lives ago.

MARY CHAY

'And besides, the wench is dead.'

The Jew of Malta, Christopher Marlowe

I

A Good Read

Unfurl my *Standard*, don't poke it
into my neighbour's eye. Or tit.
Briefcase between my calves, lest creeps . . .
This train's at Baker Street for keeps?
Oh goody, goody two shoes! Jeez!
A juicy murder's what I need
to get my teeth into. But tough

on *her*. But I've had quite enough.
I gave my humble all again,
to Hackney's under-class. The strain!
I can't believe in pure maths much –
sometimes, I think it's just my crutch.
(And if there's anything below
my year 10s, I'd as soon not know.)
Sometimes, I crave some kind of light

relief. A P.D. Rendell might . . .
Ruth James? Still dearie me, all those
pages to turn . . . I feel my toes
curling at this sad sister fleeced:
'VICTORIA MURDER . . . police
have not so far identified'
– that word can tingle my old hide –
'the body of the woman found'
– that one will run and run and – bound

to! *Ev'ning Standard* come up trumps
to life me up out of the dumps!
Every good girl deserves a treat! –
'strangled in back-water Hugh Street . . .
no handbag, but a Faber book . . .'

– some Aussie novel, clever crook! –
'. . . suspect a mugging that went wrong . . .'
– human? How much do *thieves* belong? –
'A passer-by who didn't stop . . .'

So what's a right-on mugging, cop?

Suspect

'I'd like to help you, officer, but can't,
would that I could! Walking along Hugh Street,
I didn't see or hear anything . . . odd . . .
I often troll around Victoria
after a t-t rip round clients there,
I t-t old you – you have got me down.
I mean you've got me t-t aped. Sh it –

I'm not what you are thinking, f-f uck!
I'm in computing – here's my card. I I

I feel you are regressing me right back
into the womb . . . d-d ark of that cave . . .
I n-n ever crawled out to be framed.
D-d-d amned. I am . . . Christ, c-c ram
me in here much more, I'll play b-b all –
Yeah! Yeah! Yeah!'

Forensic God

Lies are wind. In the laboratory,
the comparison-microscope waits
to enlarge on your in-truth-never-guilt-
but-inadequacy, by weighing a numbered hair
of your head, lighter than sparrow-

fall. In the balance with a possible pair,
on the face of it as way-out a match
as the unionist Major and Dafydd Wigley
covering each other
in absence from the House, *fons*
et origo of the law, whose corporeality's

the wool-sack. Cleared non-animal, this hair
from the scene of crime mustn't *snap*

with the 'suspect's' to find you wanting
. . . the verdict you always shamefully knew
from rootling around in short trousers
would be confirmed one day. Immutable
as risky pussy's pain at being stroked

the wrong way . . . overlapping mini-scales
of the sheathing cuticle
point as ever to the hair-tip, snail
growing-point. This cuticle, ghostly inter-
face of the trinity

of onion skins that's a hair,
has already proved itself
not too thick for humankind, not

the hair of a beast. Never

mind the finer points
of given identity in DNA

profiling: *under your nose and third eye too, I am*
in a cell, life-sentenced
by tell-tale roots

plumbing under-privileged
soil. If life no longer hangs on a hair,
the quality, the quality?

At The Plumbers' Arms

Above pub trestles, that plaque on the wall's
re. Master Builder Cubitt's marshland re-
development toward Victoria . . . all
leased from Lord Grosvenor, Mr Big, pre-
  Reform-Bill – '32 . . . Stucco's cracking,
like form . . . (They'll list the 1970s'
  bête noire for goggle tourists, by hanging

baskets' November evergreens? *Here is*
where Lady Lucan ran after He slayed
Nanny.) That plaque marks that old two-bar blend:
the footmen, grooms not mixed with butlers, trade.
So everything becomes quaint in the end:
old love, old art, old artisans, old death,
old crime, old form . . . sunlit, we broach new breath.

On the Clapham Bus

1. *Omnibus*

In the Thames, there's no reflected glory

of the tarty *lumière* of the Palace
of Westminster and other classy erections
– blocked by the angle of this bus, this bridge or me
as we're thrown together, a huddled mass
given over to our worries, crossing our legs on our losses.
Behind us like the *longueurs* of Vauxhall Bridge Road
. . . the emotional murders we survived or handed down.
Under our feet . . . a watery grave. So
we jolt through this May-warm November night
toward the next anti-Maestricht paragraph
or *The Sun* keening *Victoria strangler's victim*
or the summer or the summer before last's

. . . back window-box of straggling rosemary and thyme.
 Vauxhall's
always a bridge too far for me, up-stream from summer
and Lambeth Bridge, the river all lit up
reflecting . . . riding to a-light
at the scrubby roundabout for St-Mary-at-Lambeth's
churchyard. Our sunset tryst with wild pale fox-gloves and white
bunny-flowers. Our tease with the Middle Ages language of
 flowers
and Galileo's 'grand book, the universe'. Our tilt to be . . .
snowy Darby and Joan on their shaded bench . . . 'You

understand some middle-aged tinting the fifties . . .
After the war, Queen Anne's lace down green lanes . . .'
The shadow of a fox-glove spiking from a grave
slab on the ground bayoneted her crotch:
'Your man on the Clapham omnibus was always
nicely lower-middle class. Within the pale.' In truth,
whatever you say say nothing . . . In memory,
her black hand cups a pink

unofficial rose. 'Our soldiers also died
against Hitler.' Now on this bus, my neighbour's fortnight-old
poppy
blazes for the bloody soil

. . . also encompassing the Tradescants' graves
under the fuming air, with worms of worms
of their flesh feeding the soil that feeds
the pink and white mock 1600s' garden
at St-Mary-at-Lambeth, for Charles I's globe-trotting Gardeners
who discovered plants *à la Columbus.*

2. *November Garden*

The garden tells me I am dying now.
The last rose, limping to the light, heart-stops
beyond the high-noon glory of old Junes'
sun-show . . . *Sub rosa,* rust nasturtiums sprawl
drunk on late rain, spinning lush full-moon leaves.
Regeneration in the air? Too late?
How can the fat seeds form, ripen to spring . . . ?

November poppies douse one perfect rose.
Red poppies' and white poppies' bloody stain
blacks out Arcadia – just who bought that?
On my street, life's the shops' shrilling arcade.

Look to the February light of spring?
When rosy, puffy Valentine hearts come

on pasteboard, satin-padded blush . . . recycled
with shaming rhymes and ageing, baby thoughts.

3. *Calvaries, Pas-de-Calais*

Over the hedge, the green and dun, the Carse of Gowrie
through that fraying rose-bay willowherb. Walking home
from work, my thoughts wool-gathered on any thorn
. . . like a long lost letter, like most
friends'. Thirty odd years back – *après*
memory – he'd written me, roundly looping
along the lines: 'And Tim, Sunday, my boss and Madame drove
me
to Belgium, *après la grande messe, bien sûr!* First
World War land, also the French
side. Anonymous named graves, the towns'
names, St Omer, St Pol, St . . .
recognized. Only the country
lets you forget. '63. The calvaries . . .

here, in the fields outside Calais, they somehow
comfort, like the old hymn *Christ*
in a workman's jacket. Or
it's a residue of the bleeding

tears of so many believing fools, bedewing
the silly baa-Lamb face. Who looks at most slightly pained,
as if His cup of tea were cold, peeping
over hedgerow old man's beard
or fool's parsley (even in Scotland
I'm no botanist), lost in the phallic
flare of seed on a breath,
a breeze?' I'd read it as his arty-farty way, not
to say his airy-fairy style, not
looking to another to lift my yoke:
always taking the first step, making
the first move, never to be met half-way – till Lil
years later. That awesome burden
of the '50s male at the Saturday night hop
or even student parties, initiating everything or damn
all . . . some caveman travesty of personhood – till Lil

who's dead. I scrabbled for hand-holds on the earth's flat
face. Seeing above that Perthshire hedge

where old-school 'Wee Free' shadows still recede,
above a clump of willowherb half seed,
a misty calvary. And would root it up
with my bare nails.

Suspect

'. . . Aw nae.
Jeez bluidy Christ, dinna puke owre me!
Because I pissed mysel, laddie, ye think
I am a cunt. Och let me tell ye, mate,
my bladder's weak. I've had a chill aa week.
Sleepin out's nae sae guid for seniors.
And I cud be yer gran-faither, ye ken.
Yer couthy uniform wadna appear
sae braw, laddie, efter a few nichts out!
I'm tellin ye. I've tellt it ye afore.
I dinnae dae it. Can ye nae hear that?
Shite, I wis dossin doun twa streets awa
owre the Woolworth grill. I heard damn aa.
. . . I'm *speakin* English, mebbe nae pan loaf,
guid auld Queen Bessie's English. R'n P.'

Playing the Part

Walk out of Waterstone's, still

on stage, a copy of

Carey's *Oscar and Lucinda* under my arm,
like her. Neutral eyes gun for me –

blue-jeans, thick navy jersey, short
fair hair and damned

white scarf, spot on. I'm her
to a T in the November evening's
all-consuming murk, and bloody

ache. How did this one make it
past my professional portcullis? She's under

my skin. Last night, I dreamed this
bleeding walk . . . Turned off

her true route at Old Compton Street
to brush against her in that side-street crowd, walk on
together. Keep to her true route now, straight on down

Charing Cross Road, where they watch me – duck

and weave across Cambridge Circus, anonymous. Silver Moon
Bookshop, where she maybe window-shopped the good

minute that day, shuffling
into dead sisters' shoes, 'other men's flowers' . . .
sucked underground down Leicester Square tube,
with one more safe exit before the last:
WPC playing murderee. Re-

construction of bloody X's
last appearance. But I
don't feel her

. . . like that. And besides, the girl is dead.

Always a First Time

This isn't happening to me. 'Tisn't

real. I'll wait a while. Later,
blasé, I'll look back over my shoulder
up Charing Cross Road to this May-warm
November night. Where I'm stood up

at the wrong time, wrong street
corner. And my sweater doesn't fit . . . my face

doesn't fit . . . my hair . . . Jesus, I lack

street cred. And should be at Piccadilly.
I'll always remember that 1940s novel hinting
at the Dilly . . . I was scared

of kind of intruding . . . Scared

they'd suss me out – unlike the punters! –
at twenty metres, push me out
for trespassing on their patch.

That woman's eying . . . me. Blonde, blue-jeaned,
Waterstone's bag in hand. Hope she's not

a plain-clothes cop. Play pretend

looking up at the plane tree leaves:
a handful of bronze change on a midnight blue

back-lit screen sky. If I get picked up

by the cops . . . If
the man won't . . . If – *Don't*
dilly-dally on the way . . .
I'll wait a while. On the wrong street

corner. 'Yes? . . . OK, yes. Yes.'

A Detective-Inspector Donates His Body for Anatomical Examination after His Death

No. God, no. What a *billet doux* to hazard on
in the glove compartment, tempting the crash . . .
How could St Chris, swinging on childhood's blue

medallionesque, out-magic the final form
from the 'London Committee of Licensed Teachers

of Anatomy'? Lying in wait on this midden
of Mars and Galaxy wrappers, not done do-its undoing me,
an off-white mitten, God help me, if I were a man
that would be a condom . . . *To whom it may concern* – God,

society's Santa faith: somebody will be
concerned . . . future will be.

Isn't the lab's shamefaced demonstrating skeleton
plastic now? In the shoes of a London

anatomical committee-man, I'd dictate *whom*
will fucking have to heft my stiff, pick up
these pieces – since bleeding Sarah won't. So

what if X is strangled in Belgravia – or Balham –
if your ex fucking ex won't get her finger out
to shove your stiff?

                    This engine can't idle on for ever.
If nothing gives . . . An accident at Trafalgar?
Not my pigeon.

                    No bird

in my hand . . . *parts*
of special interest . . . Oh yeah

the cowed cock: after working on some spectacular
pervert, one step forward – two steps back, home
to a homily against bad-mouthing blacks and gays
from the twin bed. Jesus wept. Give me five minutes free,

I would.

... parts of special interest
for medical, educational or scientific reasons to be kept
for a limited time ... How long can it be abused and be

functional, on parade, with it,
buster? Maybe no blindness, but all those small hour calls ...
At my age and not lying down, of course I'm prostrate ...

'par for the course', as Kevin gamely quips.
At least this solves the funeral problem: you can't

see Sarah rising to the occasion, if
rolling in the aisles

at the back of me. She says ex-wives don't bury their spouses.
Don't they, hell? Divorcing

unilaterally – fledgling white-coats

will assail my too too solid ... with first-night nerves
and cutting one-liners ... Especially the little girls, learning
to cure, courtesy of my privates. Sweet
Jesus, why doesn't this turn me on, *This letter of intent*

should be kept by the donor
with either the pension book or the will. After all,

plod-plodding in my line of country,
I never looked to make old bones, even before
Sarah put in the knife.

Suspect

'. . . Aw nae.
I dinnae knife that lassie. I'm nae touched.
I've stayed in London thirty years, that's aa –
I'm nae some wee Cockney, cuttin up rough!
I'm nae some bluidy mad barbarian
rampagin aa about the warld wi bluid
trailin ahin! Like yer forefowk aa did.
Och ay. Juist ae o Jock Tamson's bairns, me.
And gettin awfu tired, ye ken. I drink
tae sleep. Jeez, sae I dae. It's the big sleep
I'm dreamin on . . . the big . . . sleep'll dae me fine.

. . . Aw nae. Aw fuckin hell. It's bluidy ye
turnin up like a bad penny again,
wi some wee touch o copper i the nicht.
I've tellt it ye. I dinnae dae it. Nae.'

Suspect

'Yeah! Yeah! I t-t old you, ev'rything
seemed normal in Victoria that night
– you've been trying to t-t rip me up.
I n-n ever knew a man would k-
k ill . . . a woman . . . round the bend, I mean
the corner. Yeah, I said that that's the way
the cookie c-c rumbles – 'cos I meant
that's life. Give me a lie-detector test.
Oh sh-sh it. You're breaking me. I had
to fight so hard to get my speech this good.
I should have been an actor. K-k ill
or cure. But you can't know, you'll n-n-n-
ever know . . . God. Why lil' me? F-f uck
. . . imprisoned by my d-d amned m-m
other tongue.'

Forensic

Here are the cells

of the medulla, typically – if present –
fragmented in a human

head hair. (Apart
from the Mongoloid continuous medulla . . .)

At the heart of the hair, the medulla's
within the outer wall of the curtaining cuticle
and the inner wall of the cortex,
whose pigment granules long dyed
a common or garden mouse. Ferociously

magnified out of all proportion,
this hair's a fallen column
from a *démodé* past,
Hellenic or Palladian,
felled by the storm or the ba-ba-

barbarians, never far off, never

mind the expansive hold-all of original sin, Gladstone
bag of muscular Christianity, imperial swag
bag. Expanded beyond belief, this hair's the trunk

of the tree of the knowledge
of good and evil – according to
the current myth, shaping up
to the gallow-tree or the tree of man,
never quiet, never

mind . . . 'Today the Roman and his trouble
Are ashes under Uricon.'
This hair bears the tenor

that that little screamer *The Sun* will print
on the bio-mass for the mass of us:

a little of what you fancy – shit
amid the shreddies and All-Bran.
This hair's that slanted column

– off-beam as men as trees, walking. Aye,
I am less a camera than a comparison-
microscope, I-ing
another 'bare, forked animal'. When isn't the end

split? Didn't the French lieutenant's woman die
in the end? We all come
to it, in the end. Common humanity?

Can't

Can't . . . in the face of a hair
on my navy cuff, coiled like a wee boa
-constrictor. Tweezer-fingers tweak

to get a grip on herself. A grey hair – so not her

melodrama. The bottle shields her:
the *vernissage* of her strawberry-blonde helmet
shining a painted saint's aureole
in the train window, where she or I see a self . . . telling

my kids, there's no such word as *can't*. But
I can't face Victoria again. Call Jake
and Claudia – but next week? What pretext for permanently
 crying

off? Isn't being a young widow enough?
If you can't out-Persephone the spring
– though I could virtually, circling
the Circle, tagging a rabbit's foot white-knight dream
– a flashing powder-puff down the tunnel

vision of the snows of yesteryear: how many snow-locked women
still fair . . . combing their tresses? She shoots

her speckless navy cuffs and knows it's not
your mind unstitching like your body. Yet

at the office, I sew things up. But can't face
Victoria. Blindfolded by the white scarf
in the photo, streaming like long white hair like
the Havisham wedding-veil-cum-winding-sheet, quick

through the underground, the rushing mighty wind
round suburban Kenton's St Mary the Virgin, with Whit blush
roses, our young wedding . . .

                                        but didn't the paper say
still evening? 'She' sees a future self tell a cop
that after the newspaper photo last week, 'I' knew
that evening I'd passed the strangle-victim in Elizabeth Street
four times *en route* to my weekly dinner with Jake

and Claudia. Doubling back to the Victoria Station Ladies,
as the victim-to-be went on dawdling to death. She gags

at the (young male) cop, seeing at best the *sportif*
forty odd young gran, who leaks if she leaps.
Sitting on the tube, she's running with her hobble-
skirt of quilted fear, faster than retired athlete
daughter Vicky, in the tell-tale snail trail
of the seventh age of age and decay that can't start, yet . . .

Can't

On the screen, for *Disk Error* read *Middle-aged Policeman Can't*
Hack It. Floored, I hunch over this word-processor, little

more than a toy for the absent child? Six

overdue letters lost. The washing-machine looms. Time
and failing way back whelped
the black dog at my shoulder, like a stole. I know
the indictment flickering marsh-fire
on the blue back-lit and night-sky screen, rising
from my damp places. In my book

inadequacy is picking up
on the right moment to sidle up to the nice man
in Dixon's, in plainest clothes,
with another problem.

I tell myself, like a fairy
story before bed,
the Victorian strangler isn't

the end of the world. Only the corpse's.

Virtually functional on a day-to-day level,
at least at work. There's no blood on the carpet

but the machine's stalled. I can't right . . .

the message on the little grey cell wall . . . Winding
in the phone-line's noose, my ex

delivered herself: 'You must pin
the Victoria strangling on somebody. Have a care
for the tourist industry. Hugh Street abuts

Belgravia.'
I can't drive the machine. Under this w.p.'s flipped
lid,

under my bonnet, lies
another country. Though at work, long computerized, I keep
    my end up
as ever. *I'd never have bought it . . .*

myself. *Chez nous*, hands on was never my style.

I can't make it on my own.
Though if I hold myself, sometimes
a memory of a hope skitters a second . . .

That's what you do in childhood
– except I didn't and she took mine with her when she left.
. . . In the sense of 'adult acceptance'? If

I clear the screen, I can't
start again. The disk's corrupt. And isn't the nature of error
penetrating the *tabula rasa*?

Dental Records

If I turn off the computer, my skull

raises its eyebrows at me, another complicit

reflection in the VDU's navy matt, dense
as the night. If
I raise my eyes to the hills, so

to speak, a regular set of reference books
is framed in the window,
in another reflection from the lab strip light
superimposing shelves of books on the dark

trees, whence they came. While in another . . .

part of the wood, trees go on
growing their dating rings. If

I think where I should be now, I think *Dear Warlock*

-Williams, except I *don't* in the end
go. To toss in my penn'orth of cod forensic
dentistry, to add to the gaiety of nations
chez not-Warlock-Williams . . . No teeth on the ground
jokes . . . my foot! No bird's-eye over-view
of sexing by a fumble round the skull's gender spectrum,
ageing by 3D-computer mapping furred-up roots
or the arcana of amino-acids locked into teeth
categorizing . . . my last

woman. Thirty. Medically healthy,
dentally ditto. Some treatment
by a Manchester-trained dentist – confirmed
by her dentist, when traced. When he named
Mary Chay. Same surname as Chris . . .

common enough? *It's not the corpse,* I'll not titillate
the Warlock's drinks-do, *but seeing the friends or 'family'*
at the inquest – that does for me, something

rotten, something on the rocks
on hand . . . Yet, when only cops and bods like me show
like this morning, I feel a moment's unease
at being

let off lightly. With a few moments'
soul-searching, like a penitential
Hail Mary, in the old country of the wooden wall-

eyed . . . we hardly know
ourselves, let alone

the other . . . story.

In Waterstone's, Charing Cross Road

1. *In Ebury Street*

George Moore's old street skirting Victoria,
toward Sloane Square. '70s route, I took
with rent each month. From here: myopia
then, not knowing *The Vivisector*'s books
except *The Solid Mandala*. Passed by
Elyot's house on pre-Blitz Ebury.
And never fossicked through *A to Z*'s lie
of that land fronting on to Battersea:
fond Eadith's brothel, seedy 'Beckwith Street'
(whence E. to 'the empty Dilly'. Bomb. He's slain.)
. . . Distant, I turned on World News – a wrung sheet,
re-reading *The Twyborn Affair* again,
book in my hand – 'Patrick White died . . .' Turned back
into the chancy page, amid the flak.

2. *On Publishing Her First Poem*

Her nostrils flare
pregnantly with the scent, the sweet
scent of success. She reviews

presentable pain, while painting her true

colours in the kidney

dressing-table mirror, holding up a self
to elusive nature. By the discard pile

of costumes, bare-ass she

dramaturges . . . nerves into lines like sound-
bites (*cedillas curtsy, serifs swoon*). The future's
scented: so

I lay out my wares, poke
of neuroses, file of guilts
– a tart at her window, above the canal
of effluent from life's pick-'n-mix
cliché free market, above the street's easy-come

. . . easy-go brutalism. Already
I'm aching . . . my hot hand
kneading the little magazine

appearances that *will* succeed, a *papier*
mâché crutch for an image.

3. ***On the Till***

Before yesterday, selling images affronted me.
Gold dust jackets beckon louder than any old Gibbon's
'street cry' – so many designer types after the latest

Amis *fils*, Will Self, *American Psycho* . . . you-know-
who, buying the right thing
for the snob reason. Though that amounts

to damn all now.
                    The cop nagged me to 'put a face
to the chit.' But we hand out receipts like plane-tree leaves.
Or a voice to the walking corpse to whom I handed it

. . . with *Oscar and Lucinda*? If

I'd delayed a second serving her – even a sneeze's
blessing – she wouldn't have been walking down Hugh Street
    then,
the strangler's eye wouldn't have bull's-eyed her,
the strangler's foot wouldn't have ghosted along
behind her – phoney shadow

entre chien et loup . . . But
some other poor sod you said,

getting it in the neck when I screamed:
some crazy *karma* or finesse of chaos

theory, microcosmic. Leaving a second later, less than
a page turning, lighter than a butterfly's wing
beating 'the unbearable

lightness of being' . . . she could've lived
(maybe no surrogate 'murderee').

My guts ribbon, bound up
with calling you again last night. A chain
of happenstance noosed

the years and choice . . . she could've lived.

On the Clapham Bus

1. *Rearing Its Ugly Head*

Always a lumpy creature . . .
So what's another lump?

What to Do after a Death, free from the DSS, waits
on the fridge. For whom it may concern,
probably her landlady, who'll conclude

she suppressed her *most personal*

effects? Hiding a self *en déshabillé*
from nosey eyes sniffing out and fingering

things and making a meal
of them, *truth to tell* . . .

precious little to trash. Last year
of National Service letters from Graham before
he met Eve. Two postcards from Reg before
he met Chris. A pussy birthday-card from Len before
he emigrated. A *Mousetrap* programme from Derek before
he remembered he was married to Désirée, who kept

the home fires burning in another part of the wood, before
she died. For all intents and purposes.
Rain or shine, she's only going through

the bloody motions. Her hospital case is her weekend
bag, left on the shelf since Guy down west found somebody

'better in bed'. So she sets her face toward
that world of flowers and visitors, killing
the long-term lonely hearts. We can't

take up our beds and walk out on the fucking couples,
the sick whose partners wait, flaring *love* in your face
till you're out cold, for good.

So Ugly stepped out, bus pass in glove, under arm
last week's *Observer*. Yet, who gives a monkey's about ex-

Yugoslavia or the woman strangled down Hugh Street

when you're on the way out?
Her last look back said: So

this was life. Reg's red rose postcard.

Death-rattling, had it the strength,
it might throw up its head

and howl at whom it might concern.

Gender went years ago
without a Tom, Harry or Dick.

2. *House of Cards*

Isn't it all luck in the end . . . the star
between Her legs flicked by His comet's tail?
And what they make of Baby, if they do?
– *sic* all of us sat on this bus tonight.
We're all victims of circumstance, in the end.
I used to wonder why folk gamble! You
make what you can of that hand dealt you, waive
your hand that deals it out . . . in next-door's lap

the *Sun*'s a blaze. That damned Victoria
strangling, hogging the head-lines, yet again
Today. Why was she there then – on the dole?
Who paid her fare? Someone paying her way?
Till 'fate' . . . The bus shuffles toward the Thames.
Westward lies Lucky Lucan land . . . The red

buses don't crash? It's safe as houses here.

3. *Semper fidelis*

From our lackadaisical herbs, the sun will cook
'hot lavender, mints, savory', cliché
rosemary for remembrance. Our garden runs
in the universal English strip, far enough out
for this in North Clapham. Yet this patch,
clematis-trellised inner harbour, ringed
by rue, with clumped French lavender, lad's love
and lemon balm . . . recalls Westminster's high
walled gardens, their old world

charm – rich cottage gardens. Honeysuckle's censed
in the dusty purlieus of Westminster Cathedral, with old roses
rarely, rarely spied from the street. From your room
overlooking next door's diaphanous pocket hanky,
a Pimlico backyard, mere and lush square feet
riot between the tall house and the wall
. . . a green shade. Feverish greenery spurts
to the day from the damp moss.

'THE SUN SAYS *Enough*

CONTACTS of strangled woman hang
back, but delay could cost a life.
Police remain anxious to trace
contacts of Mary Chay, who was

killed in Victoria last month.
Silence has lasted long enough.
Her dental records were required
to name the dead ash blonde. They said
that thirty-year-old Mary was

from Wembley Park. Workless. Shame, shame
on her contacts! The absentee
landlord knew only he got rent.
Her ground-floor neighbours said they said
'"Morning" on meeting, ONCE A MONTH.
Poor Mary needs the oxygen
of INFORMATION urgently.
Were YOU a friend of Mary Chay?
Can *you* place brave Mary? At risk
are central Londoners' lives now.
We can't allow wild beasts to roam
at will around Victoria.
Someone out there must know something.
The Sun needs *you* so's to clean up

Victoria, our country's heart.
The Sun speaks for England – the U.K.
Call our Murdered Mary Hot Line.'

Dennis Binnie Rings 'The Sun'

'Oh am I through? When I read what –
oh no, not through like *you* mean, Miss,
mustn't complain, after all life
is precious . . . What I meant's . . . Oh Lord,
when I read what 'THE SUN SAYS' said
on Saturday about the way

. . . the way 'Silence has lasted long
enough', I thought I *should* ring you,
only 'cos I happen to be

. . . an acquaintance of the woman strangled in Victoria. I
met her in Tesco. I'd knocked off a bottle
of Bitter Lemon. Plastic, it burst

a spurted silver arc – moonshine, moonshine.
Fizz everywhere – lap-

lapped at her toes, foaming. I thought plastic was safe. Don't they
say, plastic makes it safe? She said 'These things are

always slippery.' People's eyes were on stalks, which frankly
I can't countenance. Boiled beetroot,
I only wanted the shiny supermarket floor

to swallow me and my mess up. But a kind
of conversation got going, so when I saw her

picture in *The Sun* . . . You never believe
it'll be somebody close. I mean,
I've never really had . . .

what you might call a life. There was always . . .

Mum. She got ill when I left school, so
I got into caring early, you might say.
Of course, Mum had me at forty-two.

So you might say it worked out for the best
for all concerned . . . I hadn't had time

to get kids. Or a wife or anything
like that. It would be nice sometimes, kind

of going out, meeting girls and things.
Running round Tesco's one thing . . .
From the cradle, I was always kind

of shy with girls and things. But
I've not had a lot to do with the opposite

sex. Oh you've gone. Ta-ta.'

Suspect

'Passports to Pimlico – that's what you'd like!
I'm passing through. No prob? When I returned

to England, Bath, last year, I didn't *see*
Victoria. Ran down the Underground.
It's not as if I were after a youth-

ful self – which discard's that? I was . . . I am
. . . old question mark? Sure, I have hitched the world
but that's sloughed skin. Though I wrote off two lives

in two car wrecks – don't look so shocked. Two lives
out of my nine . . . Hell, once in Amiens
– so near and yet so far, yeah! *far out, man* –
with two mad Poles . . . Anything for dosh but

anything. As a student, I lived here
twenty years back. The old flower-horse stood
on Warwick Way went even then. We shift.'

Memory, Suspect

1. *Up the Line*

Even by rail – safer than road, air? – ''bye' –
after a little death, how can you bear
it . . . ? Dopey passengers straggle by and . . . ''bye'
through morning mist, where ghosts are fungoid where

Victoria's cathedral girders vault.
A penny for a candle for good or
sign me a cross for the *lares* – and taut

hanky. Chance chalked up trains to their Great War . . .

fucking graffiti, futile means and end.
Collector's gate turned Traitors' . . . uniform.
Night mail, flow safely unto journey's end . . .
in lover's waiting, nerves beyond the norm:
the sunset fires the red-coat pillarbox,
the law of averages always tick-tocks.

2. *Lhude sing cuccu!*

The BBC says summer starts today,
the longest day: in our beginning is . . .
All June the trees have see-sawed, heaven-flayed
over the square, leaching a moonshine fizz,
a timbre of old bells . . . unnerving air,
Le Grand Meaulnes' dream, old fair well lost to night

– whose wheels within wheels crank the midday glare?

. . . A fist of gnats clouds over sallow light
. . . asthmatic fume, the city's rush-hour heaves,
though I still hear a hurdy-gurdy grind.
Who leaps the spiral fire this St John's Eve?

And will he tilt at windmills in your mind?
In six creaked months, the kids sing 'five gold rings',
past the old glory, autumn barn-storming . . .

3. *70s' Tramps*

That frowzy tramp, hair buttered by the sun,
is preferable to this female drunk
whose barking ricochets off our grey gun-
metal sky. Morning booze is misplaced spunk
– she shames the rag-and-bone-man's cracked cry. Bad.
Her well-cut, puce trousers and nostrils flare.
Her record's at the wrong speed: foreign, mad

past understanding. This fury will scare?
Hatred is two-way, glanced off panes of prim
Pimlico sleeping or else peeping toms,
mewed up by net. Jerks from a silent film
– her wide flung legs, masculine, never Mom's.
Recently dressed to kill and now set to

hurry on down with swagger – in whose shoes?

EXCLUSIVE LESBO THREAD IN HUGH STREET STRANGLING

Why peer over my neighbour's shoulder to lap up
shit, as the train jolts us together and apart
behind crushed paper-thin walls, rush-houring
Northern to journey's end . . .
the Bank? My fashion journalism merely labels
the outer person in this season through
to smart fabrics – as in smart cards or bombs . . .
Not that in autumn '94, we're not

all chic. Between the tube and office, heels
clacking like *passé* typewriter keys, high-step
over jumble-sale discards
that breathe, running the gauntlet
of humanity and *Today* – up with the *Sun* – placards.
Their distorting hall of mirrors, iciest
Galerie des Glaces, less raising a glass

to nature as framing you in a phoney *ancien régime*
as emotionally non-U . . . Yet, the tabloids raise our profile
in spite of their best efforts, normalize the normal.

Hugh Street is always that day with Minette,
that last time, when I wasn't myself . . . Not
working. Afterward, into the dress-fussy St George
simply to sit down. A one-armed man rattled 'Cheer up

love – it might never happen.' Out there
somewhere, someday, there might be someone . . .
wishing on a star. But whose destiny's a career
on legs – globe-trotting, if Marilynesque
into middle age? Glossy mag job, the glam
they romanticize . . . you can't

have it all. Didn't the old proverb say God said
one wish, with luck . . . ? In the end, I trust

not very with it, like Minette passing
on in her basket between home and the Blue

. . . Cross in Hugh Street . . . that strangling. Screw
up that fishy paper, scapegoating,
and beat a spoon on her tin dish, klaxon!
for subtly brindled mousy Cat . . . Catherine
across Wembley back gardens of rose rosettes, hot lips
of snap-dragons and panda faces
of winter pansies. And hostas, hostas. 'Cath'rine, Cath'rine,
Cathy, Cathy, Cath. Cathy, come home.'

'THE SUN SAYS Hands off our murder victim

MARY molested after death.
Among today's screw-balls and nuts,
we want to say a big thank-you
to all who ransacked memory,
to call our Murdered Mary hot
line. Cheers. *The Sun* is proud to shed

its light on murder most foul, black.
Mean time, the case has been HI-JACKED
by yesterday's shock-shock report:
a woman claimed that Mary was

maybe en route to some "soirée"
(that's meeting in plain English) – those
"proselytizing lesbians".
The dead have rights – they also bleed.
Though now they rest beyond the ken
of libel laws, this need not be.
The Sun supports the defamed dead.
And what about their nearest and
dearest? They have their feelings, too.
The dead do not deserve to be

stained by sick gossip or in vogue
whims. If you want to save the dead:
Call our Murdered Mary hot line.'

'Not the country-house murder'

The street's stained, and her house, and her
insides – belly, bowels, liver, inner lights, the lot
in the formaldehyde of last Thursday
where she's suspended like a Damien Hirst

baa-lamb. She vampires the wine that *autres temps, autres moeurs,*
    is
His life-blood. This insipid sipper's sunk a red pint for starters
like a demented blood-donor at the *après*-donation: a pint
for a pint!

How much blood's involved
in a strangling outside your front door,
actually? Stranger on stranger.

Will the nasturtiums, ropey from their hanging baskets,
late, late, this Provençal November,
ever change their amber warning lights?

Come summer, the London Victoria sunlight will
lattice the strip of wall by the net curtain
of this basement dining-room, where his throat seizes up.
    Chicken

fricassé mouthfuls will repeat

now . . . the internal TV reconstruction he won't watch.
How do you puke the fowl across the intervening snow

napery, keeping face?
Virtue has gone out of this street. If
a street in spitting distance of Belgravia ever aspired . . .

Rising from table, fowl still mercifully down,
his hand touches her shoulder, but not
her . . . wanting the pure past, a couple of days

or a lifetime ago.
In passing, does a murder on your doorstep
reduce the property value?

Her parents' generation fire-watched here
for the Hun, between Christendom and the *passé* Community.
'Next week, the neighbours' – not
forgetting the funny-peculiar –

'for pre-Christmas drinks', translating: carry on
up the killing field.
'Not the country-house murder', translating:
the barbarians have arrived.

A merry little laugh from her, translating:
we hang together.

'A far cry from autism'

We 'interact', therefore we
are . . . I can't cross the room, yet

if they didn't stare so

frankly, I'd have potential for living . . . chit-
chat: 'Nothing to look at . . .' but their eyes

sucking like their lovers. Or plummy
anemones on a pool's rock-

face. I could fathom for
ever . . . the figure in the carpet,
the thin blue line, red
line . . . till the boot

fall? I've the normal hopes
and fears, like Shylock bleeding

regularly. A living doll,
who can talk
one to one. Not

a lover – I've to keep my feet
on the ground. And I'm not

further gone than the old-time girl
swooning at the swish of her dress. Only
shyness frames a looker

or half-dishy youth, more carmine
than the dress of the girl desired. Only
'interaction', the blood's mantle.

She Dreams of Leg-extenders

My problem is I can't

cross the room. My legs are
functional, but I can't
                    rise

above the level of their eyes
seeing how short and stubby
my legs are . . . *Oh like me.*

I don't fantasize legs scything
from my arm-pits or tucked up

in the lotus position. Now, the afflicted
young – like their peers, with nose-rings
and hair-extenders – are treated, with drugs
for better or worse . . . but
what of us, of 'restricted
growth' (that's far from

'dwarves'), among the stilted
middle-aged?
            These days,

I know it's *passé* to seek
to please men.

I seek to please men only
along with women and our furry

friends. Other things being
equal, I'd have aspired to be

the world's sweetheart, something
along those lines. So please
help, Marje. In your brilliant
career as agony

auntie, such small
tragedies must be

your bread and butter.
Yours,
B. Femina.

X's Column

The second-hand French postcard shows
a male smirk sucking up – down – to
some female pout, by some rose bush
beside a lych – corpse – gate, maybe
wishing well. English? – photographed
by Stebbing. Printed by Étoile
of Paris, 2 rue d'Amsterdam.
Their sepia's touched by green and pink
– rosebuds. *Emaillographie*, glazed.
The rose will soon be withered up
her frock. Her figure's an S back
to front beside her man, strong, stiff,
beside the lych gate's strong, straight post.
Fin-de-siècle dress, so he's
on stage in time for Passchendaele?
Turn-of-the-century fine hand

copper-plated *Milles Bons Baisers*
Germaine. Less lovie in French? Wreathed
under the photo over-leaf,
the sweet-hearts' couplet is pure *kitsch*
in national alexandrines:
Quand l'oiseau chante, au bois, sa cantate magique,
Vous devez de mon âme écouter le cantique.

These cards are picked up – jumble sales
or down the Portobello Road,
else with a Paris quay's *bouquins.*
En passant, as this column's stressed
re. safety in Victoria,
the victim was from Wembley Park.
Found on that girl, text just released
by the police, this unaddressed
postcard's so sad . . . The dole, without
close friends – a wild beast finished her
half-life. Spelt out . . . below Germaine
on that French card – it made me weep,
wishing my lowly column flashed
a pillar of fire bringing God,
bringing the bum to book, to hang:
'Ever come up to the bright lights?
Jobless, but live in hope. Mary.'

My Pet

Now that letters have stopped,
in my better moments I cogitate why they ever called

writing 'spidery'? Arthropodal jointed legs
ape the ghostly in the down-stroke of G, up-stroke of D?
And am I to locate among the spider's
eight simple eyes an O,

an organic O? G-spot
of the entertainment of agoraphobes, prisoners
of conscience and crooks, sharing their shrinking cells,
their sweaty house-room – if they're
'lucky' and not also arachnophobes –
with something along the lines of *Tigenaria*

gigantea, commonest of native
house-spiders, no bite, like the other Brits. Who,

at my last bath, modestly withdrew
to the slit where the white tiled wall abuts
her corner of the bath's ledge – uniform, old-fashioned
white. Unless her swarm of eyes couldn't stomach
the full frontal of the elephantine
geriatric *homo sapiens*.
Or the miraculously risen

humidity. What a *bouleversement*
of her micro-climate! She could subsist
some months without water, food . . . I gleaned
with my still lively little grey cells. After bribing
my Home Help to spirit me *Collins Gem Insects*.
Where I sexed her, seeing
as she was plumper than the absent male
in the balance of probabilities

and susceptibilities. Did she inch up
some *scala enigmatica* within the wall
to squat the winter on this snowy plateau

whiter than the pre-Chunnel Shakespeare Cliff?
In the nature of things, she can't know if she falls
I'd trail loo paper to hoist her from the bath's
mirage. Month after ground-down month,
she glowers on her bluff,
like a wannabe suicide
whose imagination's too lively.

Ephemerae

You've seen it all before. This catalogue
– Damart 'thermolactyl' underwear
'that warms the world.' Dear . . . But maybe not
kept here for fondling his or her tight
knitted crotch. No pussy here

in this no-garden-access, third floor Edgeware flat,
but *Know about Cats* from Spillers. Pussy's off

in the garden of roses, geraniums and salvias
photographed in the blaze

the free seed catalogues could be. And
newspapers, paper-bags, flyers and God help us
an invite to St Mary the Virgin's Xmas service plus
party for deserving lonely hearts,
where only the host's absent. And

coupons for food you'd not be seen dead eating,
burgers! Being too wanting for the cut-price life,

for the gas bill's final demand?
Natural gas couldn't cradle you
in the kiss of the spider-plant:
a few dun leaves blowing in the wind
on impossible steppes of worn carpet.
With Japanese koi carp swimming to the wide blue

yonder, beyond their tank on the mantelpiece
– advert 'postcard' from Maidenhead Aquatics.
Plus worse than rotting fish
fumigating this room of normality.

I glance at my colleague. We trail

the blazing scent into the bedroom, the
cunt of a corpse.

On the Clapham Bus

1. *The Land, the Land*

They stood on a low hill, a Middle
Age conquest. (I won't say
where. We don't,

do we?, now we're three
billion souls or so beyond
the pale . . .) The illimitable sky . . .

the common-or-garden grass merging in mist

in the old lie of the land. Through
the cold war earth, lesser celandine thrust

before the shortest day: come

March, a splatter of gold.
She said 'Not going, going

– it's gone. England, you know,
the country.' He said 'Lost her bloom, like

you.' A silver halo *en brosse* patted
a slumped rump. Was this ever
a land fit for heroines?

2. *Urban Myth*

Not olde corn circles or some hood who haunts
a tumulus . . . The urban myth's the one

who got away. The man driving this bus
does not deploy a talon for a hand.
There's street-cred immortality if you're
Gran on a car roof-rack crossing France, dead

till like things falling off a lorry's back . . .
Anon cream raincoat, I sit on the bus.
I didn't mean to do what I did – tugged

the V of her white scarf, a wedding-car's
crossed bow . . . But time is on my side, in the end
forgives – who cares which old-time Vandal did
down which? Unless the land dies . . . halting daze

. . . uniting time and space, too quick by far.
Still, in the long run, everybody's dead.

3. *Rubbing along*

The bus takes one step forward, two steps back.
Still, unlike the ship of the desert, it won't kneel
to that yellow man in a wheelchair. If
you look like the back of a bus, you look out

for the other, apart
from the others . . . under your skin
and on board, as the bus jolts
you any which way
                    cater-cornered
over the grey heads, bob-bob-bobbing along

to the farther shore, as old
Mother Thames runs softly, softly . . .
But at least I've kept out of the drink
so far. 'Do I deserve credit/for not having tried

suicide . . . ?' 'Good night, sweet ladies' on Vauxhall Bridge

on the 88, 'thy eyes look to me mild . . .': by chance sat by
black hair, blue-jeans, anonymous cream raincoat
and the inevitable lover to go home to? Anybody's

. . . a face for the pick-pocket's inner
pocket. A pick-up to take home like a take-out,
brimming memory's glass, to help me make

'a thing of shreds and patches'
another could call a verse? And
so to bed, by dialling somebody who
-ever lonely out there, hands across the sea, her hand
my hand across the thirsty bay. Rub, rub, rub-a-dub.

Suspect

'. . . Not going round in circles more than life –
I meant to test the chemistry of "self"
against Victoria's façades, old set
familiar once as back of my hand . . . stone.
– And I've kept mum about Cathy to keep

her out of this . . . Spur-of-the-moment gush,
calling at her old Hugh Street flat, fat chance . . .
A guy said "Charlwood Place, p'raps?" Where she gave

her kids tea. "Keep in touch", the last thing said . . .
Twenty years on, who's not shocked at that knock?

Enough to see a supermarket now

under another name . . . cockles stall gone
from Warwick Way, fouled up by the EEC?
You know I'm not the strangler, officer,
I only came to rubber-neck my past.'

Sunbathers, Victoria 1974

Under the warder eyes of tenements
all over town, forms of undress parade
themselves, airing forms of our fantasy.
But won't these pink and white limbs soon be dirt
specked by the atmosphere's smut, though we're clean
air zoned? Through rain-cloud sky's sheet metal, jags
the ragged robin skyline of down-town

a stone's throw from Victoria. A rich
scent, olive-oil sun tan, wafts cruising flies:
it makes them high, then knocks them down and out.
Did spikenard, once expended, draw gnats to
Simon the leper's house and the abased god
head? Creepy-crawlies rouse the living flesh,
embalmed with dreams of *House & Garden* life

and young bronze gods. The dozy girls are laid
mummified, baptized back in flaming June.
Why did Victorians leave 'sun-roofs', low rear
extensions of this-worldly stucco homes,
now multi-occupied? Below my pane,
lie two night-shift and blowzy belles who mustn't
uncurl a toe beyond their rug or they're

nothing but pussies on a hot tin roof.
Carapaced-turquoise, one small beetle studs
a burning thigh, falls sheerly from this bluff
in our flat world, turned upside down, to spin
a shifty gem – her friend lunged, fails to grab.
Jade with a cut look flashes faster still
. . . while from the roof of our warm world, the sun

sparks in her off-white smile a Midas touch.
A ritual exacts sacrifice. But burnt,
even scarlet . . . tender extremities
would spoil the image – red-neck cheesecake plumped
down in the market, free for all the wasps . . .
The sleepers lie on till the thunder breaks,
calling us back across the sands of daze.

Reared sheer to one-time servants' rooms, the wall's
now snaked by fire-escapes. Sloughed, wrap-round skirts,
sweat shirts – spring sales' pale discards – tart up, torch
the drab surround, the sky, an air that seeps
out of lie-lows squeezed by the surplusage
of grilling girls with brief bikini briefs
and hothouse dreams of summer before last.

Sun, that frazzled noon office lime strip-lights,
from evening sherry's gold light transmutes
Burgundy red sky over the West End.
A breeze, tinctured with cooking-oil and sweat,
breathes from the swarming royal parks and lifts,
with flying ants, brown people homing from
the cut-price, supper round-up from back yards.

In Waterstone's, Charing Cross Road

1. *Gallows Humour*

In their rows, the shelved lives . . .

I see-saw on my dilemma, in Waterstone's. How come
I, never scanning the print for black characters

or female ones, for identification,
dither like some Victorian swooner, created in the image

of the lord? A self says: Play, play to your luck,
life rarely throws up a chance, never a second. Chance

half a life-time sorting
a game of consequences? A second self says:
Play safe and grow old with the dream's
memory, laying a long shadow on the green,
green grass of home

that never was. In 1995, I'd be the first black face
in his village . . . The colonizing instinct isn't developed
in me. In his modest house of substance,
from where we'd commute to the city and the City, I fear
the *châtelaine* mode, the master key
nudging below my belt.

Yet, he'll read, mark, learn, and inwardly
digest the enNobeled Morrison's *Jazz*, my Christmas-tree
make-weight gift, beside a flashing fairy
light. I never wanted any man like him.
And yet, when I watch the magpie in his penguin suit
– one for folksy sorrow? – strutting his stuff
across his lawn, in my eyes I'm hung as a class

traitor. One of his first lessons was to translate 'black comedy'
to gallows humour: through the welter of unfortunate-to-say-
the-least
phrases, blackmailing . . . blacklegs, black days, black despair,
all Thatcher's children must be in the black.

2. *Outsider*

More cash, less cash, this class, that class
– the plot's always the same, my arse!
At work, bar, party, A meets B
providing sex, 'a new-born me'
. . . the good minute or till a crone?
Till C arrives – B's dream, B's *own*

baby. So B-and-C. Rage, rage
from A, who takes out on the page
all his/her *schadenfreude, angst*, rue.
That's takes it out on me and you,
enduring readers, who maybe
never had any chance to be

half of a pair – although so keen,
unlike A, hack writing-machine.

And why can't A and A's *confrères*
spare all us lonelies their affairs?
(Though what makes A's dear cronies wriggle
is always good for empty giggles.)
But characters like us aren't seen
in print, on stage or silver screen.
This is the message my heart thumps,
the agenda they will always dump.
I can't remember any book
where any character not crook
works through a life alone to death,
too lonesome for another breath.
That's why this bookshop makes me puke:
to the ugly, art is a rebuke.
Why can't one poetry book come out
without love poems, sexy bouts?
This bookshop – for the Everyman fluke – 's
the beautiful people's arty souk.
On hearing that word *love*, I reach
for my sick-bag. While every peach-
skin is desired, uglies are made
lonelies, whose place is in the shade.
Flush uglies, whose purses don't fail
making quite free of love for sale,
may die of AIDS. While all long-term
lonelies have suicide as germ.

3. ***On the Till***

It could be you I feel all the time
hustled from hoardings, less tarty
than the gold dust jacket fantasies we sell. Or
bounced off head-lines, overlooked
on the safe-as-houses red double-decker,
suspended between earth and hope
on a further bridge of sighs, over

the suicide river – or God . . . *Metropolitan*
Police remain anxious to trace
contacts of Mary Chay, who was

strangled . . . Victoria . . . The last . . .
If you have come to half-suspect
Mary's half-written postcard found
on her was destined for yourself,
you *are the lost link in fate's chain . . .*
Their *finger of suspicion* points . . . the slender one

in a thousand odds against being . . .

murdered. I hear her in the deep heart's drum –
Mary Chay murmuring thanks for the book

though she's bought it. I hear her in the shell

of each phone call, drowned in each
busy-busy customer's eyes, if
they look . . . Perhaps, my eyes were the last
she looked in normally . . . apathetically.

She changed my life
as if she'd tossed a coin and I'd called –
'29

. . . that's too young to be obsessed with a stranger's
murder': Brad first spoke to me in Whitehall
on the 24, my face livid with dying. Still,
in this queue at my till, I sense her

slight ghost, I couldn't flesh out for the cops . . .
beside that brown man, mauve suit, mini-Christmas tree.
While the fuzz on the back of my neck's still pricked up

at my life resolved like the spin of a coin,
like one of Brad's pots, thrown on his wheel.
My tombola womb will deliver the goods. Quick

clay, love turned and fired . . . his Chinese mother and
needing . . . his baby. Isn't the natural course
rushing from death to life? Brad swears
his internationally acclaimed pots can carry

us: I pray . . . the genetic dice are kind. We walk on

egg-shells through to funeral urns.
Is the bottom line who pays, eternally?

A Detective-Inspector Makes His Will

Down the grey shopping street, the short gold
fantasy dips into the red.

Why are the lights always against me? All
down the Harrow Road to Kensal Green,
through last century's dimly terraced industrial
outcrops. But improve the shining hour,
peek at the solicitor's draft: *I . . .*

hereby revoke all former Wills and Testamentary dispositions
made by me and declare this to be my last

Will . . . Sarah changed, not I.
The lights have been against me everywhere. Don't

let the blood boil, bringing on the blue

light out-streaking green, amber,
red. Isn't it a plus to arrange your affairs,
unlike some customers . . . That ageing hippy-type

cleared forensically. *Victoria strangler prowls on.*
I'd have put money on that hippy-type. Christ.
It comes to something when the week's high's

your will. Posthumous potency! *I give, devise*
and bequeath . . . all my real
and the residue of my personal . . . half
to my ex-other half. If they blow it

on AIDS-types or some donkey-home, what the fuck?
If she has step-kids, I'd be their sugar daddy.

. . . and to stand possessed of the residue . . . the National
Trust. Who doesn't mourn England that closed
on Sunday, with Judaism – after all, our spiritual forefathers –
our most exotic faith. – At last, the light, the clear

run. To a broader Green Belt. Victoria secure.
And the big houses standing for something. *In witness*
whereof I have hereunto set my hand
this 16th day of March one thousand nine hundred and

Let a Hundred Flowers Blossom

'We thought it was our moment . . . you know
how it is – cometh the hour, cometh

the person. And our twin life
blossomed after we met in '88, we kind
of felt we had a lot to give . . . we wanted to share . . . this
moment

in history. It was our thing. In a kind
of latter-day flower-child way – who doesn't mourn the image
of the '60s? Out of the blue

a lab colleague of Leila's asked to hold her hand
after her farewell do! We'll call her Daisy. Daisy
was leaving to have her husband's baby. Leila'd been out
for ever. She said she identified with the Merry Monarch, being
touched
for the King's Evil. Daisy didn't even want a kiss. Leila gave
a contact number. 'Ideal Home' young wife. For baby's sake

she'd not drunk.
Then, in our fullness, we wanted to be there for a few
Daisies. Leila put up a note in a bookshop re. Thursday
soirées for 'women confused about their sexuality'.
Two straight friends helped. Leila had a kind
of image of a bowl of Japanese paper flowers opening
in water. I teased her as not-the-green-fingered gardener.
Whacky,
your silence says? But for some we had something. For some

had nothing. After the murder down the street,
I told the cops about our *soirées* for fear a victim could be

en route to us – sometimes women phoned who never showed.
Though not that evening . . . We were linked to the strangled

through fear, alone . . . After the press door-stopped us, Leila
wanted out
to start again in another part of town. I was

paralysed. The sunlight of publicity picks up
the hair-fine crack, not like the line on a nasturtium's petal
in our old garden . . . Not like you, not the serious press
after the issues . . .' *. . . bit-part victims of this stark crime:*
Leila Purcell's presence is still
felt in a flat along Hugh Street,
doors from the murder, where her ex,
Gwen Brown, now lives alone . . . Behind
sad window boxes, wreathing still
last year's forget-me-nots, black, blown . . .
A shadow of her former self . . .

Nasturtiums

Promising more light for 50p.
than that coin in any blooming meter,
30 Woolworth's seeds like 60s' beads, *never*
failing . . . For once, the gurus know
their onions, fool-proof for fool's

gold. Red gold. All summer

the rain raggle-taggled them,
but in rare sun they flare. High

summer, you don't notice back-up buds replacing
bulky seeds returning to the soil,
to light next summer . . . you

don't notice until
the suckers seize the ground

. . . the day. Until the frost's first last kiss
in the garden's micro-climate of cold
war. Then they sprawl in greenery-yallery,
a compost heap that's all their own
and studded with seeds chunky as dried chick-peas.
And when the leaves have gone the way of all . . .

fleshy-wan stalks criss-cross
the ultimately burning earth: a pale design
like hot-cross buns'. *Lucky Strike* seeds store shades
blood-red through jaundice-yellow.

Conviction

They must've bloody forensic stuff on me?
If you're in spitting distance of a crime,
they've got the goods on you today. Poor me,
trusting to bourgeois camouflage, my part

-time job. Two-timer . . . My mind's meshed, Queen Mum
hat veil, through know-all shrinks' *intrusive thoughts*.
If I'm short-fused . . . who lit the fuse, old God?
It's programmed in at birth, like root-blonde hair.
If she'd not tried to hold on her handbag,
I wouldn't have to live a lie, fear dreams.
And chemically what's free will, God oh?
Mapped genes are bolstering Calvin's regime,
though predetermined damned fuse with elect . . .
The future will white-wash me? And, mean time,
no one can raise the dead. Dear Christ, not yet.

Another Story

And besides, the girl is dead. And
he hooks back the receiver. And looks past
the black dog on his shoulder, nobody
waiting . . . If not now, when?

Silly to ogle the phone wire's noose, question-

marked . . . But why does it feel like grassing on
your sister? But what if another sister's cut down like a flower
of the field . . . The BT notice printed black on white is skeletal
trees, recalling that Perthshire graveyard's thatch of snow
on soil . . . But what if they don't believe you? But what if

they do? He's through and starts to blurt
and wants to pee and reads his piece: 'I saw

a woman carrying a white scarf . . . bundle it'
– sounds like a bloody new-born baby, whose *love child*? –
'into a Sainsbury's bag she grabbed from the gutter'
– *gutter-snipe* crows from some forgotten midden –
'at the 88 bus-stop on Vauxhall Bridge. Victoria-side.' Again, some-
thing white scrunched in a fist fixes his nosey eyes,
he'd looked for knickers blooming, some sort of slip. A white
scarf's feathery tassels did damn all for him. Bliss-

fully ignorant that in a *mauvais quart d'heure*,
a white scarf had become London's least desirable accessory.
More enflaming than any old white feathers. 'That

evening of the Victoria strangling.' Spastic,
the phone cord tweaks an old queen's yoke; history's
dog-ends under-foot in the pissy booth – plus his story
ending in the usual way, like hers . . . 'And I've seen her

on the 88 since then, the Clapham bus.
I maybe should've phoned before but my girl-friend'
– maybe should've said wife? – 'died from cancer and I was

up in Blairgowrie with her brothers but that's another story . . . Yes . . .
yes.' After the tests and hospital, the interviews and court? If
– it's only if it's bad news 'if' means 'when'?,
whatever's bad news now . . . this side the breeding bomb.
If they pin it on the woman on the bus forensically, he'll be star

witness? Christ, the press. He wants to run

and burrow his face in any lap.
They'll fossick in his wound for ghostly copy.

II

Portobello Road

Cheaper than newspapers, at 20p!
Fig-leaves for everyone, plus the odd flea!
I ease it off the rack . . . and *so* myself,
promise of summer . . . *moi* in my new pelf!
Here at this off-off-Portobello shop,
monochrome afternoon, November town,
beguiling transformation bids you bop
amid *démodé* hems. Yanked up and down,
some second empire line . . . It came and goes

to hang clashed, slashed, outside this shop, *Retro,*
a stone's throw off the pastel-stuccoed hill
down where the Portobello Star sails, still,
into the city of dread . . . druggy night.
Dive down the tube, Hades' hole, shake off light,
whorled through that dress's pattern, Paisleyite.

Whorled

In my Boots bag, the dress: the night-sky ground's
punctured not by the stars but Paisley whorls
plumped into caterpillars curling round . . .
or white cats, circular. The lithe train stalls
straight out of Notting Hill Gate, Porto bell-
o – beautiful harbour, Columbus' name
in their new world . . . Flea-market frock, old *Elle* . . .
goes jigger-jig around my lap . . . old game,
bone-shaking to Victoria, safe home.

That black girl stares, she doesn't see the slip
of summer-short sleeve teasing from the lip
of plain Boots bag: a lemon, seeping foam,
ghost of old sweat round one white whorl. Old fling
. . . underground, circling royal parks, the spring:
I'd touch Her hem and feel my cock, rising.

Green Park

I smooth my skirt, here at the fence, the sea-

green Green Park, *grass of home* . . . where you could drown . . .
Victoria – someone staring swallowed me.
I ran back down the escalator, down . . .

Esprit de l'escalier v. ball-breaking eyes?
Ball-bearing . . . Still, I can't enter the park,
London's green lung's not now my ur-womb ark.
The spreading chestnuts . . . and the grass – I shy

away . . . away, one tube stop, spewed up here,
bodkin eyes are anyone's plain clothes fear.

I miss the Sunday 'sketches' by the rails
. . . memories *doré* of Green Park, for sale.
I mourn that green mantle against the gale:
a-wearing of that green . . . we crossed the park.
A quicker spring . . . and we, any two sparks.

The Army & Navy Store, the Ladies

Gonna wash that man right out of my hair . . .
Washed up in here, my too large hands soft-soap
– but aren't we all gonners, given 'nough rope . . .
pearlies, *full fathom five . . . she loves you! Yeah!*
The swing door swings, some she will come – some belle!
Blue-jeans and jersey, white scarf – something spills

– blouse button. (Heads or tails, when either's nil?)
I grovel for it, know my place . . . my Dell-
eresque squeaking voice . . . 'Hi!' ('Bat out of hell?')
'Pretty pendant', she points after her thanks
between the loos and basins, other ranks . . .
It bounces on my boobs, my outer heart
of falsie bosom, all my showy art:
white blouse with shell-pink English roses, rife.
I stagger from the Ladies into life.

Composite

On this shop floor . . . this old department store,
my eyes magpie, if not through black and white
but autumn Day-glo, fed consumers' *more* . . .
Yet, there's a white scarf floating on the light,
finely toothed tassels and sheerly silk sighs . . .
Always 'a thing of shreds and patches', spry
I walk the plank . . . to some *démodé* shawl
– a game of consequences. Aren't we all?
Where is the tissue . . . paper patterns' stall
for dress-making? Mum was a girl with wings,
a paper Virgin . . . rearing like a swan.
Memory's dressing . . . an Angel of Mons?
Cubist insight or *origami* thing?

Recall Matisse's photo: wheel-chaired, snip-
snipping the jazzy paper, bare foot slip-
slipping toward fall.

Fear of Sighing

Their eyes are cutting . . . like on dotted lines.
They size me up, like guts for garters – mine! –
outside the Army & Navy shop – whoa!
I'll mingle (dust to dust – Artill'ry Row)
down Greencoat Place, down Greycoat Place, the fork

of tell-tale tongues froth-frothing as they talk,
getting their end away . . . *wher'er you walk*
down streets I know back of my hand, old show:
Wilfred Street, Francis Street and Vincent Square,
Elizabeth Street, Cath'rine Street, Will-ow

Will-ow Street, oh how often I've to tear

around the corner, any bad girl – hee-
hee! Scared of my two big feet tripping me . . .
And scared of sighing, though *dressed* that's my part
– or was, when Woman was a work of art.

In the Club

Toes on the kerb, like talons on the ledge . . .
here where cracked stucco is a chancy hedge
for freaked-out traffic, other . . . worldly chrome.
Anywhere over Vauxhall Bridge Road's home.

Rochester Row's behind me . . . where I raked
around the later knocked-down Gents. Else quaked
by Churton Street's flared 70s' gay club,
twin bitch damp noses twitching . . . falsie bubs.

A plummy drape is drawn by memory
on *moi, flâneur*-ing for the life of me . . .
Don't darken that door, where you mightn't be

what is required? Arden face mightn't fit
and as, sweet Christ, for that tart skirt's gashed slit . . .

Yet May, two floors above the common, Di's,
I had not known that people lived so . . . high.

Cornucopia

What is within this glass has saved my life . . .
cream velveteen with orange blossom, rife,

black straw hat on a barley-sugar stand
– a plastic twist – amid wild silks, *voile* and

I once waltzed in, simpered and trousseau'd through
after some coffee 'lace' creation, frou-
frou frothing over giantess feet . . . Shoo! shoo!

Stray domino blinks darkly at me, bride . . .
eye slits are sky are thigh – a dummy's side.
Second-hand *Cornucopia* is my pass!
I touch a hem – and what the fuck the glass!
Old boy's nose pressed – and what the fuck the farce!
Across my smocking breast, outside the shop,
bowed peasant, plus cart, all his roses' crop,
tramps on and on until the day we drop.

The Flower Horse

. . . Some place, some anon street like Warwick Way,
Victoria's everyday, the pavement grey,
between the nose-to-tail cars walking on . . .
outside Tesco, the flower horse stood on . . .
Back twenty years – still more, somehow consumed . . .
springtime for Hitler, with the stall's perfume.

Above the cart's cut blooms, pit ponies loomed . . .
how it is . . . like that 70s' nag's rheum.

Who said the world's . . . upon a turtle's back,
pre-west-regarding-mapper-Mercator?
Who put so many of us on the rack?
Marginals, pendant from the globe, gone cracked . . .

under that horse's right hind hoof – no more

lifted as if to scratch the tarmac's black
all day, before he took sick . . . flowers back.

'Black Marias'

Down Warwick Way, grey street, grey, they passed on

mid afternoon, toward dear life's next con.
I didn't know I'd seen them, but I felt
the running stitch of their peeled, guarded, eyed
. . . eyes morse-coded along the van's black side:
each mail-box slit, two eyes. White, black . . . fate dealt
. . . and God knows if 'free will' does take a hand
bringing us down, bone-shaking by and 'bye . . .

wrist-vein blue as that old remembered land . . .
high-rising to that blue men call the sky.

(And Boston's 'giantess Negress'? – M. Lee,
first 'black Maria' . . . used by stressed-out cops,
to yank the bolshie cons, court to cop-shop . . .)

Despite myself – two Is – two eyes, trailed me,
releasing me – hard, in four walls. Then tea.

Pendant

So memory has served to buoy me home
here where I'm at . . . my Egypt – Athens, Rome.
My hither-thither heart returns to 'norm'.
If nothing else . . . wanking keeps me on form.
My pendant lies across my Snow-white front,
'Pretty' pretty she called it – can't I shunt
her out of mind? Why her? Girls walk the streets
twilight . . . it wasn't too late in the day?

My pendant looks like frozen pee, ripe-wheat,
gross amber tear – no flies on me – oh say,
I'd pined the *Rosenkavalier*'s fey,
wry silver rose . . . found this in that Crusaid
shop, Upper Tachbrook Street, whence all my frayed
Edwardian magazines, with dog-eared peace,
frothing dust's pollen . . . that last summer's lease.

Old Monthlies

Mortality's old binding gone to seed,
handful of dust, Eve's black mischief, white mis-

(chief, that's pre-'20s, pre-Second Wave . . . His
story officially.) *The type you read . . .*
Bound vol *bouquin*-ed in Pimlico for Her,
this *Englishwoman* fading into fur
of dust of 1912 . . . whose dreams recur
of better lives or even the good life
not *sine qua non* Someone's lovely wife . . .
Mrs. Henry (Suffrage) Fawcett on the age,
'*The* shoe for dancing' (Drew's) opposite page,
the Cinderella Sewing Machine Co.,
plus 'Improved Knitted Corsets' or '*Tricot . . .*'
I hide my bloody balls under my best
dress – not to be a cuckoo in the nest.

Moth-balled

For ever and a day, to keep your head
down . . . here, milking my silks and glam-puss rig,
the fig-leaf apron glad-ragging the figs . . .
I fantasize Hurt Duffield in hot red
butterflyed, 'skied' within the wardrobe's dark
. . . no lion, witch, kiddies in that Christian ark.
(*The Vivisector*'s former flat – *quelle vie!* –
Ebury Street, beyond Hugh Street, crow-flight,
is now next door *The Lion, the Witch and the*

Lamp-shade, antiques!) Bushy-tailed and eyes bright
among my raves, my faves, my lights, P. Whites,

everything's tinctured *v.* the dowdy moths
nib-nibbling knitted dream . . . field of the cloth
of gold . . . Of leaves of camphor, volatile . . .
by sublimation, purified . . . High style!

Bearing Witness

And so I sit and stew in old days' sin
over my books, their voices' dizzy din,
lie of the Gothic type, a style ago . . .
Washed up from our history's tacky show
my tat clothes, tattier – pre-'Great War' – mags,
my regular monthlies, bloody glad rags . . .
Damned skewed? Not Beaumont Soc. T.V.s' right-on
upstanding membership, even *la bonne* . . .
Sure, I've psyched up a *self* (who he?) to drop
be-jeaned, all fine and dandy, round the cop-
shop . . . shopping *moi*, if . . . if a conscience-sop:
'I saw her in the Ladies on the day

she died. Christ, officer . . .' quite how to say –
and what of colleagues in the Revenue?
I didn't see how I could see things through . . .

III

Hugh Street

Fuck! Stone the crows! Stone me! Christ . . . did I think
this quiet street today would be a sink?

The very stones do not cry out, and why

should they? Granite-hearted . . . and you? And I
about my lawful business round the town . . .

I didn't bring a posy to cast down,
screwing a red, red rose, until it bled

paradise . . . petals, gorgoned to dead head.

A puddle, where the spilt petrol reflects
a slaty pigeon's rainbowed, heaving neck,
cradles the illegitimately dead.

A murder here a year ago. That day
I met that face the papers say . . . that day . . .

I grovelled piggy for her in the dirt
. . . a pearly button off her cheese-cloth shirt.

'THE SUN SAYS *Remember, remember*

LET'S SPARE A THOUGHT for Mary Chay.
This dreary, dark November-tide,
we've celebrated Guy Fawkes Night
and Poppy Day, let's now recall
Mary, *The Sun*'s own murderee.
Remember, white scarf strangle-ee?
Star of our Murdered Mary blitz
campaign, two years ago. *We won!*
Her killer skulks in prison now,
lucky to have a life at all.
We ought to honour all the dead

who've fallen in the War on Crime
as, proud, we say *We can take it.*

In all our busy lives today,
let's clear A LITTLE SPACE for her
so animally, evilly
strangled in quiet, staid Hugh Street,
Victoria, our country's heart.
Here's looking at you, Mary kid!'

Hugh Street, Again

Shock of the same . . . stucco'd houses, two rows.
(Near Belgrave Road, don't grope and hitch my hose
under old Chelsea-look full dirndl skirt!)
Last year's anniversary . . . yesterday:
autumn, same quiet street, same pain inert
– only a page turned over, dashed away

as ash. And what would dead Mary have made
of two more years of days, these books of hours?
Routinely, Middle Age makes two years fade?
Nessa Bell-esque *après* Dorelia's shade,
accordion dirndl concertina'd show'rs
flowers on her *tombeau*, as might have been . . .
Near stranger, I've cast Mary: friend. Who'd seen
through 'dangly bits' under my skirt – no squeaks!
Flash of white petticoat, old-Missie-meek . . .

White Poppy

Glimmering in the autumn gutter – rose,
white poppy? Only snotty tissue blown
down that dead end, where's coolly disclosed
the once familiar frozen music, stone;
the lone gas street-lamp, fêted years ago;
the same black paint and cracking white stucco,
the same cracks plastered, playing peek-a-bo!

A few November steps down Tachbrook Street,
the market in the road's only a beat
up-market. But that greengrocer, Med-blue
eyes, navy wool gloves with the fingers cut,
mental arithmetic speedster, has shut
his stall. Other folk? Twenty years on, who
knows? Twice-Ulyssed, does time *mean* for you?

All that has mattered to me happened here,
started . . . Green to return, the scene . . . so near

the past? Dusk falls. Victoria's white walls rear.
A dirty British pigeon's butting to
and fro; around the wobbly neck, the rain-
bow's draped. A ruddy blur lights my old pane,
and I'm a ghost aching below . . . I'm who's

leaning against the wall, once shop, deep, dense
with third-hand furniture, tat for old pence –
opposite *Migrants Resource Centre* now.
I dragged a desk across the street somehow,
and bamboo bedside table, ten bob, thence.
Through dusk, I see in that room, clear as day
the green, green grass of home whereon I lay

. . . the landlord's greenery-yallery rug,
after the basic, purest, only drug . . .
banging my head to make pain blanket pain
and pick the bloody poppy, sleep, again?
Face down the day – and mail – and so keep sane?
And I'd Canute years, bring back yesterday,
the BBC says summer starts today . . .

Yes, yes, as Mollies of the world would say
– not only Dublinesque, feminine, gay.
Wasn't the heart's rôle always to crash the mind?
Across the rug, I saw curled melon rind
my ship of death . . . Yet, that was life. And love
across the miles from London, as the dove
would fly . . . And both of us tried to be kind . . .

Too bad to be picked up – briefly – as – prime? –
Chay death suspect, when I was out of time –
gin in re-named 'Elusive Camel', limed
in past: *love is in town, with trysting light*
in eye . . . two baby-boomers stroll with white
pacifist poppies, grey November day.
From where I never leave, I walk away.

In the Cells

You think that I'm a leper . . . that I am

beyond the pale . . . on a lower plane.
I too have felt . . . the sadness of the last

pale rose of summer, some November plot . . .
And then, I've sat beside you on the bus,
the 24, the 29, of course
the Clapham 88. We're all in it
together on 'the omnibus' – if one
or two minus a right-on gene or two . . .
Minus imagination, God help you!
Still, in the long run, everybody's dead.

The future will acquit me, why not now?
I said I didn't mean to kill the bitch.
Not *Killed for Kicks by Part-time Private Nurse.*
Mugged. Once, my life would have hung by a thread.

White Scarf

1.
'Oh Mummy, wouldn't it be fine to be

wrapped up like some silk-worm in his cocoon?'
Out of the mouth of babes and sucklings . . . Free?
This 'ordinary' rain-lit afternoon,
'But you are safe, my dear . . .' flesh made by love.
At school these days, what is it that he hears,
bombs bowled through stories . . . death lobbed from above?
Silk is for future frocks, parachutes . . . Sheer
– forget the silk-worms, burning to serve us –
like that white, tasselled scarf my sister gave

to her inept young man, who'll without fuss
go up to guard the sky . . . another grave.
Christ that my lad wore leading strings. Not brave.

2.
Is this what it was for? Those years at school,
learning to parse dead languages. To lie

under an English elm, old view . . . young fool
to watch them take the view away . . . To die.

Is this what 'Hare and Hounds' race truly meant?
Whither their trail of blonde confetti bled?
– a dog-fight over hop-fields of Kent.

What price their neo-pax-Romana? Red –
I'd kiss May's white scarf if not for blood's stench.

Figures . . . of loss do not add up for her . . .
You do it 'cos – how not? No matter, wrenched
by 'God', by guts, by li'l' Mr. Hitler.
Mulishly, you go up to die for her.

3.
'Gawd, 'ave an 'eart, guv, where're you comin' from?
"Recall" one bloody bag "by thinkin' back"!
Till IRA cease-fire, I checked for bombs –
it's lookin' for a needle'n an 'ay-stack,
not that some needles ain't so rare today.
And we ain't paid to poke round carrier bags
– bums droppin' trash for us to sweep away.
Big deal some strangler's mixed with them toe-rags!
But we don't look for Oxfam scarves inside
stinking old bags – they crawl – would make you *swoon* . . .
Sad that another li'l' lady died,
let's 'ope that white scarf shows up some blue moon.
Jeez, ain't we livin' in a strip cartoon!'

4.

The news blows past me . . . in tears, down Kingsway . . .
a thing of shreds and tatters, flesh and war –
or pads me out between greasy wool, frayed
White-scarf trial witness hangs himself – 'No more.'

Didn't I see it blowing in the wind

. . . a bonnet's long white wedding ribbon, taut,
snaking the gutter from a bag not binned.
I could have picked it up. Perhaps I sought
the pretty . . . flimsy thing, no warmth. All sorts

of magpie instinct for what's going free . . .
'What's in yer fuckin' bags?', they scream. 'Old bag!'
I rock on, side to side, scream silently
What's in yer pants then, young pin-stripy lag?

Rockabye

On, on to the end, I would rock on through bright lights, and dying
when *rosé*-blush first light is steeping tight sky towards Stepney . . .
Up-beat as I can be, not tetchy and wretched and whingeing.
Like sheep? – we've to count up our blessings. And shrug off self-pity.
Sweet Jeez, I'm alive! In these days of the white silk scarf strangling

that drew us together, for ever I felt in my fullness . . .
Brad saw me upset on the bus, though I wasn't a witness
through serving *her* hours before, Waterstone's bookshop. I threw up
that job, as he bore me away amid sobs like fierce hiccups

and we were an item then on . . . . to the latter-day swaddling
of you, as it were in white silk, a man's '30s scarf blowing

as Brad was soon breezing right out of my life, short-lived
    rapture,
my safe old job forfeit. Inspire me and keep me, love, going
on, on. On *far out to the shallows and straits of the future . . .*

Detective's Story

Mustn't nod off . . . in this steel jam.
Don't cuddle the steering wheel.
The rattle in the engine's in my head, yet . . .

not a bad way to go . . . driving home.

Look bad. Yet, they'd say
On his way out.

Going west, the wind-screen wipers bat the rain
like eyelashes. The anonymous

vicinity of Brent Cross. You soul
search if the Industrial
Revolution shouldn't have been strangled
at birth . . . In the after-life of retirement, how

would the day-long office hours pass? Reading
Ruth Rendell plus the TV cops?
A little charity? In the toxic after-
glow of a Nonconformist conscience. Trial

run for the big sleep.

Switch on the radio, switch off the lies.
Even now, their voices come at me –
colleagues', coroners', cons', courts', cells'. And Sarah always hitting

the spot (*G-spot, love. Find it, one day*).
The voice asserts I, I, I
. . . as much as any thumb-print that's been in it.

Voice-printing'll soon have us all taped,
scatter gun or lilting, personal rhythm

as if there were any rhyme or reason
in it all. At least, I wasn't shot. Win
some, lose some, before you lose

it. Pray
the Chay killing isn't my last high

profile win? (And not with namby 'psychological'
what's-it!) That killing's a candle in my skull:
we brought the Chay killer to book.